The Rejection of Palestinian Self-Determination

The Struggle for Palestine and the Roots of the Israeli-Arab Conflict

Jeremy R. Hammond

Copyright ©2009 by Jeremy R. Hammond
All rights reserved.

ISBN: 978-0-557-09569-8

Contents

I. Introduction 1
II. The British Occupation of Palestine 3
    The Rise of Zionism 4
    The Balfour Declaration 8
    The King-Crane Commission 11
    The Churchill White Paper 14
III. The Palestine Mandate 19
    The Hope Simpson Report 21
    The Arab Revolt 25
    The Peel Commission 28
    The McDonald White Paper 32
    The Arab and American Positions 38
    The Anglo-American Committee of Inquiry 40
IV. The U.N. Partition Plan and Arab 'Catastrophe' 48
    Zionist Terrorism 58
    The Birth of a Nation 60
V. Conclusion 67
Notes 68

I. Introduction

No serious discussion of the Arab-Israeli conflict can take place without an understanding of its root causes. The ongoing violence in the Middle East must be understood in its historical context. There is often a tendency to dismiss the past as somehow irrelevant. Elsewhere, there is acknowledgment that the facts of history matter, but accounts given rely heavily upon historical myths and other distortions.

Given these tendencies, it is little wonder people watching the continued violence on their televisions often give it little consideration. There's nothing that can be done about it, many have come to conclude. Many succumb to the myth that Jews and Arabs in the region have always been in conflict, or that there is an innate enmity between the two peoples. Others simply resign themselves to the belief that the conflict is inevitable, that the situation is too complicated to be understood or for any practical solution to be found.

This book sets out to show that these are mistaken beliefs, that by correctly identifying the conflict's root cause, it becomes simple to understand. And from that understanding must follow rejection of the view that the violence is inevitable and there can be no solution.

It is well beyond the scope of this book to provide a fully comprehensive account of the history of the Israeli-Palestinian conflict and its origins. Rather, the goal here is to dispel a number of persistent myths about the conflict and establish through examination of the historical record that its root cause is the rejection by Zionist Jews, Great Britain, the United States, and even the United Nations of Arab Palestinians' right to self-determination. The discussion of this period, from World War I until the creation of the state of Israel, will focus largely on key historical documents to examine the roles of the players involved and the nature of the policies they chose to implement.

The argument here begins with a number of assumptions. First among these is that the proper framework for discussion is not a state's "right to exist", but a people's right to self-determination. Second, it is assumed that Jews and Arabs share equal rights. Finally, it is accepted as a further truism that the rights of neither people should be prejudiced.

An examination of the history of Palestine leading up to the creation of the state of Israel reveals incontrovertibly that these truisms were in fact rejected by policymakers who had the power in their hands to decide the fate of the region. It is the thesis of this book that it was this initial rejection of the rights of the Arabs, as well its manifestation in policies and actions that continue even today, which is the root cause of the continuing conflict in the Middle East.

II. THE BRITISH OCCUPATION OF PALESTINE

During the First World War, Great Britain and France contrived to divide between themselves conquered territories of the Ottoman Empire. Under the Sykes-Picot Agreement of 1916, it was decided that the French would control the territory that today includes Lebanon and Syria, while the British proclaimed for themselves Palestine (a region today including Israel, the occupied West Bank, and the Gaza Strip), Transjordan (now Jordan), and what is now Iraq. In an effort to characterize their division of the territorial spoils of war with an air of benevolence, the two Allied nations stated under the Agreement that they were "prepared to recognize and protect an independent Arab state or a confederation of Arab states".[1]

The British also encouraged the Arab revolt against the Ottoman Turks. Implicit in their support for the Arab struggle to gain independence from the Empire was that they shared that ultimate goal. Explicit support for Arab independence was also declared. Six months after having occupied Jerusalem, for example, the British government announced that its policy was consistent with the goal that "the future government of these regions should be based upon the principle of the consent of the governed".[2]

Such declarations were intended to gain the support of the people of the region by convincing the Arabs that the British both recognized and supported their right to self-determination, but were really part of a cynical and duplicitous game designed only to help ensure British hegemony over the region. Captain Thomas Edward Lawrence, who came to be known more popularly as "Lawrence of Arabia", famously encouraged the Arabs while telling his superiors that the revolt would serve Britain's purpose by helping to break the Middle East into "small jealous principalities incapable of cohesion".[3]

THE RISE OF ZIONISM

At the same time Britain was making promises in support of Arab independence, there was a growing movement among European Jews to establish a home for the Jewish people in Palestine, the historical location of the Biblical nations of Israel and Judea. This movement, known as Zionism, had begun to take root in the late 1800s. The leading Zionist spokesman of the time, Theodor Herzl, had recognized that in order to establish a national home for the Jewish people in Palestine, the resident Arabs would need to be relocated. "We shall have to spirit the penniless population across the border," he wrote in his diary in 1895, "by procuring employment for it in the transit countries, while denying it any employment in our own country. Both the process of expropriation and the removal of the poor must be carried out discreetly and circumspectly."[4]

The following year, Herzl published *Der Judenstaat*, or *The Jewish State*, in which he outlined his ideas for "the restoration of the Jewish State." "The whole plan," he wrote, "is in its essence perfectly simple.... Let the sovereignty be granted us over a portion of the globe large enough to satisfy the rightful requirements of a nation; the rest we shall manage for ourselves." He proposed the creation of "The Society of Jews", which later became manifest in the World Zionist Organization.

The Rejection of Palestinian Self-Determination

The question of location came down to "Palestine or Argentine?" (Uganda was later also considered). Palestine was preferable since it was a "historic home" for the Jews, and if given the land, they could "undertake to regulate the whole finances of Turkey" for the Sultan, "form a portion of a rampart of Europe against Asia, an outpost of civilization as opposed to barbarism", and safeguard the "sanctuaries of Christendom".

The interests of the Turks, Europeans, and Christendom were thus accounted for. Completely absent from even the slightest consideration were the mostly Muslim Arab inhabitants already living there, who constituted the majority of Palestine's population. Herzl did note that "the emigration scheme" would "inevitably" rouse "many deep and powerful feelings. There are old customs, old memories that attach us to our homes." But he was speaking of the Jews who would leave their homes to relocate to Palestine, not of the Arabs whom he intended, as part of the scheme, to "spirit" across the border. Arabs, one would have to presume, had they actually received any acknowledgment of their existence in *The Jewish State*, must have no such deep feelings or any particular sentimental attachment to their homes.

Herzl also proposed the creation of a "land-acquisition company."[5] To this end, the Jewish Colonial Trust Limited was created by the Second Zionist Congress in 1898, out of which evolved the Jewish National Fund (JNF).[6] The JNF would buy land from Arabs, but never sell any back to them. Arabs would not be hired to work on land purchased by the JNF. The Constitution of the Jewish Agency for Palestine signed on August 14, 1920 stated that "Land is to be acquired as Jewish property . . . to be taken in the name of the Jewish National Fund . . . [to] be held as the inalienable property of the Jewish people." Colonization would be promoted and "it shall be deemed to be a matter of principle that Jewish labour shall be employed", to the exclusion of Arabs.[7] Some Arabs sold land to the Jews either for personal gain or debt-driven necessity, but the practice was generally frowned upon within the Arab community. The total area owned by Zionist organizations and Jewish individuals by 1948 amounted to less than 7 percent of Palestine.[8]

Moreover, under the Ottoman Land Code and Registration Laws of 1858 and 1859, people who had lived on and worked the land their entire lives often found themselves disenfranchised. Under the first of these laws, the State effectively claimed ownership of the land and individuals were regarded as tenants. Individuals could gain land privileges by cultivating, in which case the unproductive tenant's claim to the land would be forfeit. Subsequent to the Land Code of 1858, further provisions allowed for individuals to register for a title-deed to the land. But the requirement to register was largely ignored by landholders. So long as they could continue to live on and work their land, they saw no need to register, and thus only did so when they wanted to sell. Moreover, there were incentives not to register, including the desire to avoid granting legitimacy to the Ottoman government, to avoid paying registration fees and taxes on registered property, and to evade possible military conscription. Making matters worse, land lived on and cultivated by one individual was often registered in the name of another. Whole villages were registered in this manner, oftentimes with the local government magnates filing for the town, resulting in city authorities having the land of others held in their names. Most of the land "legally" purchased by Jews was from large landowners, including absentee landlords, resulting in the eviction of many Arabs from land that was by right their own.⁹

Many years later, Israeli Minister of Defense Moshe Dayan commented on this early displacement of Arabs, saying:

> We came to this country which was already populated by Arabs, and we are establishing a Hebrew, that is a Jewish state here. In considerable areas of the country we bought the lands from the Arabs. Jewish villages were built in the place of Arab villages. You do not even know the names of these Arab villages, and I do not blame you, because these geography books no longer exist; not only do the books not exist, the Arab villages are not there either. Nahalal arose in the place of Mahalul, Gevat—in the place of Jibta, Sarid—in the place of Haneifs and Kefar Yehoshua—in the place of Tell Shaman. There is not one place built in this country that did not have a former Arab population.¹⁰

According to noted Israeli professor and civil-rights activist Israel Shahak, these villages were "destroyed *completely*, with their houses, garden-walls, and even cemeteries and tombstones, so that literally a stone does not remain standing, and visitors are passing and being told that 'it was all desert.'"¹¹

To achieve their goal of establishing a Jewish state in Palestine, Zionist leaders appealed to Great Britain. Herzl had already suggested that the proposed Jewish state could serve as an "outpost of civilization, as opposed to barbarism." Chaim Weizmann, another leading Zionist, wrote in a private correspondence in 1914 that "should Palestine fall within the British sphere of influence, and should Britain encourage a Jewish settlement there, as a British dependency, we could have in 20 to 30 years a million Jews out there—perhaps more; they would . . . form a very effective guard for the Suez Canal." In 1916 Weizmann wrote that Britain "would have in the Jews the best possible friends" who could "serve as a bridge" between the West and the Middle East, an argument that in itself "ought to carry great weight with any politician who likes to look 50 years ahead."[12] Such arguments succeeded in garnering sympathy for the Zionist cause within the British government.

THE BALFOUR DECLARATION

On November 2, 1917, British Foreign Secretary Arthur James Balfour sent a letter to financier and representative of the Zionist movement Lord Lionel Walter Rothschild that contained a declaration approved by the British Cabinet. The declaration read:

> His Majesty's Government view with favour the establishment in Palestine of a national home for the Jewish people, and will use their best endeavours to facilitate the achievement of this object, it being clearly understood that nothing shall be done which may prejudice the civil and religious rights of existing non-Jewish communities in Palestine, or the rights and political status enjoyed by Jews in any other country.[13]

This statement, which became known as the Balfour Declaration, was cited by the Zionist leadership as a means of granting legitimacy to their aspirations, which had been

The Rejection of Palestinian Self-Determination

reiterated by Lord Rothschild just a few months prior, on July 18, in a memorandum that expressed "the principle that Palestine should be re-constituted as the National Home for the Jewish People."[14] Any opinion the Arabs might have about their homeland being so "re-constituted" was of no consideration.

Chaim Weizmann further revealed the prevailing attitude towards the Arab population of Palestine in commenting after the Balfour Declaration that "with regard to the Arab question—the British told me that there are several hundred thousand negroes [sic] there but that this matter has no significance."[15] In a letter to Balfour in May 1918, Weizmann wrote about "the problems which confront" the Zionists; namely the Arabs, who "worship one thing, and one thing only—power and success"—unlike the British and Zionist leaders, who apparently lacked any such negative character traits. The British, Weizmann continued, know "the treacherous nature of the Arab" and must take care not to "give the Arabs the slightest grievance". Arab "screams", such as those heard following the announcement of the Balfour Declaration, were due to "misinterpretations and misconceptions" about it, including the Arab fear that the British would "hand over the poor Arabs to the wealthy Jews" who were "ready to swoop down like vultures on an easy prey and to oust everybody from the land".

With such fears attributed only to Arab paranoia and delusion, Weizmann proceeded to shower the British with flattery, describing them as "fair and just". An Englishman's "only guide in this difficult situation is the democratic principle". Elucidating on his interpretation of "the democratic principle", he explained that since "the brutal numbers operate against us, for there are five Arabs to one Jew", therefore the "present state of affairs would necessarily tend towards the

The Rejection of Palestinian Self-Determination

creation of an Arab Palestine, if there were an Arab people in Palestine"—the implication being not that no Arabs inhabited the land, but that they simply didn't meet the criteria for being considered a "people". The Arab Palestinians were either racially inferior or lacking qualifications for nationhood (or both). Since this was the case, Weizmann added, no "Arab Palestine" would arise. The Arab majority "will not in fact produce that result because the fellah is at least four centuries behind the times, and the effendi . . . is dishonest, uneducated, greedy, and as unpatriotic as he is inefficient." So the views of the Arabs may be dismissed and their right to self-determination rejected.[16]

While expressing their support for the Zionist project, the British at the same time sought to reassure the Arabs. A joint British and French declaration in 1918 stated that their objective in the region was "the complete and definite emancipation of the [Arab] peoples and the establishment of national governments and administrations deriving their authority from the initiative and free choice of the indigenous populations." Recognizing the self-contradictory policy of the British government, Balfour told Zionism's most influential supporter in the U.S., Supreme Court Justice Louis Dembitz Brandeis, that this "complicated" the situation, but not to worry; "Palestine", he explained, "should be excluded from the terms of reference because the powers had committed themselves to the Zionist programme which inevitably excluded numerical self-determination."[17] In other words, the policy of Britain was, with only the slightest pretense to the contrary, explicitly rejectionist.

THE KING-CRANE COMMISSION

While Zionists represented a minority among Jews, the inclusion of influential figures such as Weizmann and Brandeis among their numbers allowed them to effectively lobby in favor of their cause. Weizmann had managed to persuade Lord Balfour, and Balfour in turn assured Brandeis, "I am a Zionist." Although in the minority among American Jews for supporting Zionism, Justice Brandeis was a powerful figure in Washington who advised President Woodrow Wilson to lend his support to the creation of a national home for Jews in Palestine. Wilson had earlier expressed sympathy towards the Zionist cause during his campaign, and in 1918 publicly expressed his "satisfaction" of "the progress of the Zionist Movement" since the Balfour Declaration. While most American Jews were anti-Zionist, many evangelical Christians believed that the restoration of the Biblical state of Israel was ordained by God, and even that this coming to pass would usher in the return of Jesus the Christ. But even as support for Zionism gained a foothold in the U.S., government policy towards Palestine remained ambiguous.[18]

To determine just what the positions were of the various parties in the Middle East, President Wilson proposed a commission to be headed up by Henry Churchill King and Charles R. Crane. The King-Crane Commission report of 1919 observed that the British had made conflicting promises to the Zionists and the Arabs. With regard to the self-contradictory Balfour Declaration, it stated that the creation of a Jewish state would inherently constitute "the gravest trespass upon the 'civil and religious rights of existing non-Jewish communities in Palestine.'" In discussions with Jewish representatives, far from being simply a perception among Arabs resulting from unjustified paranoia, "the fact came out repeatedly . . . that the Zionists looked forward to a practically complete dispossession of the present non-Jewish inhabitants of Palestine, by various forms of purchase." Noting that President Wilson had laid down the principle of self-determination as one of the ends for which the Allied powers were fighting during the war, the Commission determined:

> If that principle is to rule, and so the wishes of Palestine's population are to be decisive as to what is to be done with Palestine, then it is to be remembered that the non-Jewish population of Palestine—nearly nine tenths of the whole—are emphatically against the entire Zionist program. . . . [T]here was no one thing upon which the population of Palestine were [sic] more agreed than upon this. To subject a people so minded to unlimited Jewish immigration, and to steady financial and social pressure to surrender the land, would be a gross violation of the principle just quoted, and of the people's rights, though it kept within the forms of law.

Muslims represented about 80 percent of the population and both Muslims and Christians were "practically unanimous" in their opposition to Zionism, the Commission reported. Despite having begun "the study of Zionism with minds predisposed in its favor," after examining the "actual facts in Palestine" and considering the declared U.S. policy of supporting democracy, the Commission recommended against

The Rejection of Palestinian Self-Determination

favoring the Zionist goal. The claim of the Zionists "that they have a 'right' to Palestine, based on an occupation of 2,000 years ago, can hardly be seriously considered." Furthermore, British officers consulted by the Commission agreed that the Zionist goals could not be achieved "except by force of arms." The Commission concluded that a healthy regard for the principle of self-determination "would have to mean that Jewish immigration should be definitely limited, and that the project for making Palestine distinctly a Jewish commonwealth should be given up."[19]

The recommendations of the King-Crane Commission report, however, were rejected, and the report itself was not made public until several years later when it was published in *Editor and Publisher* and reprinted in the *New York Times*. The full text of the report was accompanied by an editorial introduction that criticized the fact that it had been suppressed for so long. The report "makes clear the glaring contrast between the solemn pledges of the European nations to the peoples of the Near East and their subsequent imperialistic course", the editorial stated. The report also showed that the people of the Middle East had been looking to the U.S. for leadership and protection. Popular sentiment had favored the U.S., which was respected and reputed to be fair in its dealings. But their hopes were betrayed when the recommendations of the report were not implemented. "Looking backward," the editorial continued, "it now seems rather guileless of President Wilson and America and the little nations to have assumed that the facts of international conditions should determine conclusions."[20]

Considerably more guile and entirely different assumptions were employed by others to arrive at wholly different conclusions. Balfour himself observed that the British leaned more towards Weizmann's interpretation of "the democratic principle", noting in a memorandum to British Foreign Secretary George Curzon on August 11, 1919 that the British policy consisted of "flagrant" contradictions between promises made to involved parties, but that this should be of little concern:

> For in Palestine we do not propose even to go through the form of consulting the wishes of the present inhabitants of the country, though the American [King-Crane] Commission has been going through the form of asking what they are. The four great powers are committed to Zionism and Zionism, be it right or wrong, good or bad, is rooted in age-long tradition, in present needs, in future hopes, of far profounder import than the desires and prejudices of the 700,000 Arabs who now inhabit that ancient land.

No declaration had been made by the British with regard to Palestine, Balfour added, that "they have not always intended to violate".[21]

THE CHURCHILL WHITE PAPER

One consequence of Britain's policy was increasing tensions between Arab and Jewish communities, resulting in occasional outbreaks of violence. In May of 1921, a series of riots occurred in Jaffa. Arabs assaulted Jewish communities, destroying property, looting, and murdering. According to a British Commission of Inquiry into the riots, 27 Jews were murdered on the first day of violence. The next day, there were Jewish reprisals.

The Rejection of Palestinian Self-Determination

Jews beat on the door of one house and when an Arab mother opened the door, she was shot dead, her baby wounded. In another incident, Jews broke into the home of an Arab man and shot him. They proceeded to beat him where he lay and "when his little daughter ran to her father her head was cleft by a blow from an axe." Among the examples of Arab terrorism that day, an isolated home had been attacked and the bodies of five Jews were found beaten or stabbed to death. A sixth was found some distance away, killed after having his hands tied behind his back. Sporadic violence continued in the days that followed, resulting before it was over in the deaths of 47 Jews and 48 Arabs.

The Commission concluded that the causal factors were related to Arab political and economic grievances and that "there is no inherent anti-Semitism in the country, racial or religious." On the contrary, Arabs "would welcome the arrival of well-to-do and able Jews who could help to develop the country to the advantage of all sections of the community." Zionists had propagated the theme "that the realization of the policy of the 'National Home' will benefit Arabs as well as Jews", but had "failed to carry conviction to the Arabs on this point." This was due in no small part to contradictory messages about Zionist intentions. Zionist publications, for instance, had published "provocative statements", such as the example of the lead article in the *Jewish Chronicle* shortly before, on May 20, which read:

> Hence the real key to the Palestine situation is to be found in giving to Jews as such, those rights and privileges in Palestine which shall enable Jews to make it as Jewish as England is English, or as Canada is Canadian. That is the only

> reasonable or, indeed, feasible meaning of a Jewish National Home, and it is impossible for Jews to construct it without being accorded a National status for Jews.

The Jews were not alone in making "provocative statements". An article had appeared on June 4 in *Palestine*, a publication of the British Palestine Committee that, "in discussing the question of Jewish immigration, describes Palestine as a 'deserted, derelict land.' This description hardly tallies with the fact that the density of the present population of Palestine, according to Zionist figures, is something like 75 to the square mile."

At first, the Commission had been "unaware to what extent such expressions of opinion" had been "authorized by responsible Zionists." But when the acting Chairman of the Zionist Commission was interviewed,

> he was perfectly frank in expressing his view of the Zionist ideal. . . . In his opinion there can only be one National Home in Palestine, and that a Jewish one, and no equality in the partnership between Jews and Arabs, but a Jewish predominance as soon as the numbers of that race are sufficiently increased.[22]

The demographics of Palestine were shifting steadily in that direction because of Jewish immigration, but Arabs continued to constitute a sizeable majority. According to the 1922 British Census for Palestine, 78 percent of the population was Muslim, 9.6 percent Christian (also mostly Arab), and 11 percent Jewish. Of the Jewish population, "perhaps two thirds were European

The Rejection of Palestinian Self-Determination

immigrants and their offspring—some having arrived late in the nineteenth century, others since the inception of British rule."[23] Among the third of the Jewish population that was native to Palestine were many orthodox Jews who were also opposed to the Zionist program.[24]

The attitude of the Zionist leadership towards the Arab majority also stood in stark contrast to the Arab position that Palestine should become an independent state that protected the rights of the minority Jewish inhabitants. This view had been expressed to the King-Crane Commission in a resolution adopted at the General Syrian Congress, which included representatives from Palestine. The resolution stated, "Our Jewish compatriots shall enjoy our common rights and assume the common responsibilities."[25] But this vision of a democratic Palestinian state was rejected by the Zionists and their British benefactors.

In June 1922, the British Secretary of State for the Colonies, Winston Churchill, issued a White Paper that attempted, unsuccessfully, to address the growing conflict between Arabs and Jews by placating both sides. The White Paper emphasized that the Balfour Declaration had not aimed "to create a wholly Jewish Palestine" and that "any such expectation" was regarded by the British "as impracticable." It assured the Arabs that it was not Britain's policy to subordinate them to the Jews and reminded the Zionists that the "Jewish National Home" would be "*in* Palestine" (emphasis added) and that "all citizens . . . in the eyes of the law shall be Palestinian". What was intended, the White Paper essentially said, was some kind of autonomous Jewish community in a greater Palestinian state. The existing Jewish community, it asserted, in fact had "'national' characteristics." It was this community and not a Jewish state

The Rejection of Palestinian Self-Determination

that the British had been in favor of. The White Paper observed that with the addition of 25,000 immigrants since the British occupation had begun, the Jewish population of Palestine had risen to 80,000. The British would limit immigration, but allow it to continue.[26]

While it contained language clearly designed to allay Arab concerns, Churchill later explained that the actual intention of the White Paper was "to make it clear that the establishment of self-governing institutions in Palestine was to be subordinated to the paramount pledge and obligation of establishing a Jewish National Home in Palestine."[27] And even if the British did only intend the creation of some kind of autonomous Jewish community, the end result would be the same. The Arab delegation's written reply to the White Paper protested that "The intention to create the Jewish National Home is to cause the disappearance or subordination of the Arabic population, culture and language."[28]

That was precisely the goal of the Zionists, while the British, as Balfour and Churchill had both explained, had no intention of taking the desires or rights of the Arab majority into serious consideration.

III. THE PALESTINE MANDATE

The League of Nations was founded following the First World War by victorious members of the Allied powers, although the United States notably abstained from joining. Although one of its stated purposes was to prevent further war, the League of Nations would be instrumental in helping to ignite a conflict of grave and far-reaching consequences; one that continues to the present day.

With consideration for the territories in the Middle East occupied by the Allies during the war, the Covenant of the League of Nations asserted that some communities were "not yet able to stand by themselves" and would therefore require the "tutelage" of the occupying power, or the Mandatory, as it was so called. Other communities had "reached a stage of development where their existence as independent nations can be *provisionally* recognized" (emphasis added), but they also would remain under "administrative advice and assistance" of a Mandatory. In a nod to the lofty principles upon which the League had ostensibly been founded, it was also inserted into the text of the Covenant that "The wishes of these communities must be a principal consideration in the selection of the Mandatory".[29]

Despite this wording, the Palestinians were not consulted on the selection of the Mandatory for Palestine. The Zionist Organization, on the other hand, was.[30] In July 1922, the League of Nations issued its mandate for Palestine, which recognized the British government as the occupying power in Palestine and effectively conferred to Britain the color of legal authority over the region. In doing so, the League also formally endorsed Zionism by asserting that Britain "should be responsible for putting into effect the [Balfour] declaration", the terms of which were reiterated in the text of the mandate.[31]

During deliberations over the wording, British Foreign Secretary Lord Curzon had objected that "The Zionists are after a Jewish State with the Arabs as hewers of wood and drawers of water. So are many British sympathizers with the Zionists." The "entire concept" of Zionism was "wrong", he argued. "Acting upon the noble principles of self-determination and ending with a splendid appeal to the League of Nations, we then proceed to draw up a document which . . . is an avowed constitution for a Jewish State."

Curzon later related in a memorandum that when a draft of the mandate was shown to France, "it at once excited their vehement criticism on the ground of its almost exclusively Zionist complexion and of the manner in which the interests and rights of the Arab majority . . . were ignored." Italy was also apprehensive, although both nations assented to the final draft.

Curzon was not alone. When the issue came up in the British Parliament, Lord Sydenham replied to Lord Balfour that "the harm done by dumping down an alien population upon an Arab country . . . may never be remedied". In addition to constituting an injustice towards the Arabs, "concessions" had been made "not to the Jewish people but to a Zionist extreme section". The Mandate would "start a running sore in the East," Sydenham presciently proclaimed, "and no one can tell how far that sore will extend."[32]

THE HOPE SIMPSON REPORT

Tensions between Jews and Arabs continued to escalate as a consequence of British policy, resulting in further acts of violence. In August 1929, Arabs reacted violently to false rumors that likely originated with the British-appointed Mufti of Jerusalem, Haj Muhammed Amin al-Husseini. Word was spread that Jews were attempting to take control of the Temple Mount in Jerusalem, intending to destroy the sacred mosques of Al-Aqsa and the Dome of the Rock, and engaging in massacres of Arabs. The lies achieved their apparent intent, and Arabs responded by engaging in real massacres of their own. Throughout the following week, Arab mobs terrorized Jewish communities, killing 133. The worst massacre occurred in the town of Hebron, where 67 Jews were murdered, despite the efforts of some of their Arab neighbors to prevent the atrocities.[33]

An inquiry into Arab riots was made known as the Shaw Commission, which perceived that "In less than 10 years three serious attacks have been made by Arabs on Jews. For 80 years before the first of these attacks there is no recorded instance of any similar incidents." Representatives from all sides of the conflict had testified to the fact that before the First World War "the Jews and Arabs lived side by side if not in amity, at least with tolerance, a quality which today is almost unknown in Palestine." The causes of the violence, the Commission determined, were Arab resentment towards Britain's immigration policies and denial of self-determination. "The Arab people of Palestine," the report noted, "are today united in their demand for representative government."[34]

The Rejection of Palestinian Self-Determination

In 1930, Sir John Hope Simpson was commissioned to write a report on immigration and land settlement issues. He remarked on the differences between the Palestine Jewish Colonization Association (PICA), founded by Baron Edmond de Rothschild, and the colonization that took place under the Zionist Organization:

> All the cases which are now quoted by the Jewish authorities to establish the advantageous effect of Jewish colonization on the Arabs of the neighborhood, and which have been brought to notice forcibly and frequently during the course of this inquiry, are cases relating to colonies established by the P.I.C.A., before the Keren Heyesod [JNF] came into existence. In fact, the policy of the P.I.C.A. was one of great friendship for the Arab. Not only did they develop the Arab lands simultaneously with their own, when founding their colonies, but they employed the Arab to tend their plantations. . . . It is also very noticeable, in travelling through the P.I.C.A. villages, to see the friendliness of the relations which exist between Jew and Arab. It is quite a common sight to see an Arab sitting in the verandah of a Jewish house. The position is entirely different in the Zionist colonies.

Zionist colonization, the Hope Simpson Report observed, resulted in the displacement of Arabs, contrary to Zionist denials. While the Zionists proclaimed goodwill and cooperation with the Arabs "at public meetings and in Zionist propaganda", the fact was that such rhetoric was "not compatible" with Zionist policy contained in legal provisions. While their propaganda claimed that Arabs profited from Zionist colonization, the fact was that land purchased by the JNF

> ceases to be land from which the Arab can gain any advantage either now or at any time in the future. Not only can he never hope to lease or to cultivate it, but, by the stringent provisions of the lease of the Jewish National Fund, he is deprived for ever from employment on that land.

These policies were contrary to Article 6 of the Mandate, which said the rights and positions of the Arabs may not be prejudiced in the facilitation of Jewish immigration. Moreover, the Zionists were "using every effort" to ensure that their policies were "extended to the colonies of the P.I.C.A.", with "some considerable success" already. These Zionists policies were "liable to confirm a belief that it is the intention of the Jewish authorities to displace the Arab population from Palestine by progressive stages." (Simpson nevertheless suggested this "belief" was "unfounded", despite the strong evidence he himself related showing that it was very well founded indeed.)

It was also the position of the Zionists, as expressed by the General Federation of Jewish Labor, that restrictions on immigration would violate "the inalienable Jewish right of return to Palestine". As an executive from the labor organization explained, "the Zionist Organisation gets its money from Jews abroad." This influx of capital to Jewish communities resulted in a growing disparity between Jewish and Arab education, the latter of which suffered from insufficient financing under the administrative budget of the British Mandate. There was at the time "serious unemployment" among the Arabs (though this was "regarded as a myth" within "Jewish circles"). Unemployment was due to a number of causes, including immigration. Jewish vehicles were "driving the camel and the donkey off the roads" and more modern construction methods were "displacing a large number of stonedressers and stonemasons". Unemployment was accompanied by falling wages and some laborers were "willing to accept any wage if only they could obtain work." This was "resulting in a distinct reduction of the standard of life among the Arab laboring class."

Simpson asserted that the British policy should consider unemployment in Palestine as a whole "and there must be no discrimination between the races" in Palestine. "It is wrong that a Jew from Poland, Lithuania, or the Yemen, should be admitted to fill an existing vacancy, while in Palestine there are already workmen capable of filling that vacancy, who are unable to find employment." The government's clear duty was to prevent immigration if it would exacerbate the problem of unemployment (although, he warned, "This policy will be unacceptable to the Jewish authorities").[35]

Some of the findings of the Hope Simpson report were echoed in the Passfield White Paper of 1930 (named after the Colonial Secretary at the time), which drew criticism from the Zionist Organization. In response, in February 1931 Prime Minister Ramsay MacDonald wrote a letter to Chaim Weizmann that was made public in which he explained the British interpretation of its policy declarations. The Mandate had ensured that the rights and position of non-Jewish inhabitants would not be prejudiced with regard to Jewish immigration. MacDonald asserted that Britain's obligation "to facilitate Jewish immigration" could "be fulfilled without prejudice to the rights and position" of the Arabs, without any explanation as to how this could be possible. As for the "apparent conflict of obligation", the British government must insist that immigration be limited by some measure, but that such regulations were based on "purely economic considerations", of which unemployment must be a factor.[36]

Weizmann later recalled regarding the letter as "an official reversal of policy" from the one outlined in the Passfield White Paper, which he characterized as an "attack" that had been "successfully repulsed." As evidence of the "reversal", Weizmann presented

> a simple fact: it was under MacDonald's letter to me that the change came about in the Government's attitude, and in the attitude of the Palestine administration, which enabled us to make the magnificent gains of the ensuing years. It was under MacDonald's letter that Jewish immigration into Palestine was permitted to reach figures like 40,000 for 1934 and 62,000 for 1935, figures undreamed of in 1930.[37]

THE ARAB REVOLT

In 1933, the Arab Executive Committee was formed, and sought to cooperate with the British administration. In 1936, the Committee pushed for the establishment of a legislative council as a move towards representative government. The move was quashed, however, after the Zionist Congress rejected the idea as a violation of the Mandate.[38]

The Rejection of Palestinian Self-Determination

The Arabs had had enough, and by April 1936, a major rebellion was underway. The Mufti of Jerusalem, al-Husseini, became head of a new organization, the Arab Higher Committee, which called for a general strike. The revolt prompted David Ben-Gurion, head of the Labor faction of the Zionist movement, to announce that "there is no conflict between Jewish and Palestinian nationalism because the Jewish Nation is not in Palestine and the Palestinians are not a nation", an expression of the Zionist designs on the whole of the region and rejection of Arab nationalism and right to self-determination, similar to Weizmann's remark that there was no "Arab people" in Palestine.39 Israeli Prime Minister Golda Meir later would similarly remark, "It was not as though there was a Palestinian people in Palestine considering itself as a Palestinian people and we came and threw them out and took their country away from them. They did not exist."40

Ben-Gurion also said,

> We must see the situation for what it is. On the security front, we are those attacked and who are on the defensive. But in the political field we are the attackers and the Arabs are those defending themselves. They are living in the country and own the land, the village. We live in the Diaspora and want only to immigrate and gain possession of the land from them.41

Ben-Gurion acknowledged further that "politically we are the aggressors and they defend themselves. . . . The country is theirs, because they inhabit it, whereas we want to come here and settle down, and in their view we want to take away from them their country, while we are still outside." The Arab revolt

The Rejection of Palestinian Self-Determination

"is an active resistance by the Palestinians to what they regard as a usurpation of their homeland by the Jews. . . . Behind the terrorism is a movement, which though primitive is not devoid of idealism and self-sacrifice."[42]

Ben-Gurion's admiration for the Arab determination and willingness to sacrifice for their cause was not unlike the admiration Adolph Eichmann expressed for the Zionists after having travelled to Palestine in 1937. "I did see enough to be very impressed by what the Jewish colonists were building upon their land," he remarked of his brief visit.

> I admired their desperate will to live, the more so since I was myself an idealist. In the years that followed, I often said to Jews with whom I had dealings that, had I been a Jew, I would have been a fanatical Zionist. I could not imagine being anything else. In fact, I would have been the most ardent Zionist imaginable.

Eichmann identified with the Zionists on some level, saying "there was a very strong similarity between our attitudes in the SS and the viewpoint of these immensely idealistic Zionist leaders." He recalled having told Dr. Rudolf Kastner, a representative of the Zionist movement, "We, too, are idealists and we, too, had to sacrifice our own blood before we came to power."[43]

Throughout the rebellion, Arabs were also divided against themselves. Arabs who were deemed political opponents of al-Husseini or "collaborators" with the Zionists or the British occupiers also became victims of violence. The number of Jews killed, about 500, was half that of Arabs killed by fellow Arabs. The rebellion was also forcefully suppressed by the British, who, along with Zionists and Arabs who opposed the revolt, were responsible for the deaths of an additional 1,100 Arabs.[44]

In 1937, the Arab Higher Committee was outlawed and al-Husseini fled Palestine.[45] The British put up a barbed-wire fence along parts of the border with Lebanon, Syria, and Transjordan named after Sir Charles Tegart, who proposed the idea. *Time* magazine described it as "Britain's most ingenious solution for handling terrorism in Palestine"—recognizing the rights of the Arabs and allowing the establishment of a representative government, apparently, would have been too unimaginative. The June article ended, "The fence will be completed in August, announced Sir John [Shuckburgh, Deputy Permanent Under-Secretary for Colonies]. Almost as he spoke, a band of Arab terrorists swooped down on a section of the fence, dubbed Tegart's Wall, ripped it up and carted it across the frontier into Lebanon."[46]

THE PEEL COMMISSION

During the years of the rebellion, the British appointed a commission in order to "ascertain the underlying causes of the disturbances". The Royal Commission (also known as the Peel Commission after its head, Earl Peel), in its report of July 1937, noted Britain's conflicting promises to Arabs and Zionist Jews and again found that the causes of the uprisings in 1920-21 had been "namely, the demand of the Arabs for national independence and their antagonism to the [Jewish] National Home. . . . These same causes brought about the outbreaks of 1929 and 1933." By 1936, "the sufferings of the Jews in Germany and Poland" had resulted "in a great increase of

Jewish immigration into Palestine" that "intensified" the situation.

Nevertheless, the British admired the economic development of the Jewish communities. The commission noted the "striking" differences between the Jewish and Arab communities and expressed concern that the "very different standards of living" between Jewish immigrants, who were "backed by large financial resources", and the "comparatively poor, indigenous community" might lead to "serious reactions." The commission recognized the Zionist rejection of the very idea of an Arab government in Palestine, which would be the result were there to be representative government (as Weizmann had acknowledged in outlining his interpretation of "the democratic principle"). It also recognized the Zionist insistence that "there should be no new restriction on immigration nor anything to prevent the Jewish population becoming in course of time a majority in Palestine." In other words, democratic government was fine with the Zionists, but only if Jews were the majority. The commission's report again recognized that the Zionist's goals "could only be maintained by force".

This made immigration a problem, one which was "aggravated" by "the drastic restrictions imposed on immigration in the United States" and persecution of Jews in Germany and Poland. So far, the only consideration for limiting immigration had been the "economic absorptive capacity" of Palestine, a policy that ignored "Political, social, and psychological factors", which should also "be taken into account." The report then proceeded to ignore all these other factors and recommended that while Jewish immigration should not be unlimited, it should nevertheless continue.

While a single Palestinian state in which both Arabs and Jews would "become Palestinian citizens" would be preferable, the fact was that the "Jews have not availed themselves readily of the opportunity afforded them of becoming Palestinian citizens" and had no interest in doing so. Similarly, the "ideal system of education" would be one in which Arabs and Jews were educated together on an equal basis, but the British had already prescribed separate school systems, leading to disparity and each developing its own "nationalist character" that was "incompatible" with the other. The conflict would inevitably grow worse if the status quo were to continue.

The Peel Commission thus rejected a single-state solution, British policy having contributed to making it impracticable, and instead recommended that Palestine be partitioned into separate Jewish and Arab states. This would be closer to the aims of the Zionists than the autonomous communities within a greater Arab Palestine that had been previously suggested as an interpretation of the Balfour Declaration. As for the Arabs, they would be expected simply to "sacrifice" in order to "help to solve" the "Jewish Problem" unfolding in Europe by conceding to the demand of a European occupying power to let significant portions of their land be taken over by European immigrants. This "sacrifice" would not be without reward: by doing so, Arab Palestinians "would earn the gratitude not of the Jews alone but of all the Western World", who themselves declined to offer to make this "sacrifice".[47]

The partition proposal was met with varying degrees of rejection. The 20th Zionist Congress declared that "the scheme of partition put forward by the Royal Commission is unacceptable", while at the same time expressing a willingness to consider the concept further. The Zionists had in mind the creation of *Eretz Israel*, the Land of Israel, that would not only include the entire territory of Palestine, but also parts of Lebanon, Syria, Transjordan, and the Sinai Peninsula.[48] David Ben-Gurion and Chaim Weizmann leaned towards supporting partition as a means to this end. Ben-Gurion explained that

> The acceptance of partition does not commit us to renounce Transjordan; one does not demand from anybody to give up his vision. We shall accept a state in the boundaries fixed today, but the boundaries of Zionist aspirations are the concern of the Jewish people and no external factor will be able to limit them.[49]

Ben-Gurion again expressed the Zionist "aspirations" in 1938, arguing that

> after we become a strong force, as the result of the creation of a state, we shall abolish partition and expand to the whole of Palestine. . . . The state will only be a stage in the realization of Zionism and its task is to prepare the ground for our expansion into the whole of Palestine by a Jewish-Arab agreement. . . . The state will have to preserve order not only by preaching morality but by machine guns, if necessary.[50]

Ben-Gurion further explained in a letter to his son that "A partial Jewish state is not the end, but only the beginning." Once they had an army, then the Jews "will not be prevented from settling in the other parts of the country, either by mutual agreement with our Arab neighbors *or by some other means*" (emphasis added)—presumably including "machine guns".[51]

The Rejection of Palestinian Self-Determination

In 1939, the British finally agreed to invite Arab representatives from Palestine and the Arab states to a conference in London. The Arabs demanded independence and representative government in which the Jewish community could be represented in the legislative assembly in proportion to the Jewish population. The Zionist representatives rejected this proposal. When the British suggested a revised proposal in acquiescence to Jewish demands, it was rejected by both sides.[52]

THE MCDONALD WHITE PAPER

In 1939, the British government issued another White Paper (sometimes referred to as the "McDonald White Paper" after British Colonial Secretary Malcolm McDonald) that deserves particularly close attention both for the historical role it played and the insights it provided. It stated that while the goal of the Zionists "was not precluded by the terms of the [Balfour] Declaration", it was the view of the British government that the Declaration did not intend "that Palestine should be converted into a Jewish State against the will of the Arab population of the country." Britain had already expressed its policy towards Palestine in its White Paper of 1922,

> But this statement has not removed doubts, and His Majesty's Government therefore now declare [*sic*] unequivocally that it is not part of their policy that Palestine should become a Jewish State. They would indeed regard it as contrary to their obligations to the Arabs under the Mandate, as well as to the assurances which have been given to the Arab people in the past, that

The Rejection of Palestinian Self-Determination

the Arab population of Palestine should be made the subjects of a Jewish State against their will.

As evidence that the British government had honored its commitment to the Zionist leaders and the Jewish communities in Palestine, the White Paper noted that since 1922, 300,000 Jews had immigrated to Palestine, bringing "the population of the National Home" to 450,000, nearly one-third of the whole population, up from only 11 percent just 17 years before. The document hailed the "achievements" of "the Jewish National Home", which was "a remarkable constructive effort which must command the admiration of the world and must be, in particular, a source of pride to the Jewish people." These existing communities, then, were the fulfillment of the Balfour Declaration according to the stated intent of its authors, although not at all what the Zionists had in mind.

Stating that Palestine should not "remain forever" under British "tutelage", the White Paper emphasized that the people of Palestine should "as early as possible enjoy the rights of self-government". Setting aside the proposal to partition the territory, the British reiterated their "desire to see established ultimately an independent Palestine State. It should be a State in which the two peoples in Palestine, Arabs and Jews, share authority in government in such a way that the essential interests of each are shared."

The White Paper noted "the fear of the Arabs that this influx will continue indefinitely until the Jewish population is in a position to dominate them". The "extremely grave" consequences were increasing incidents of violence, which were "only the latest and most sustained manifestation of this intense Arab apprehension". The terrorism committed by some Arabs "against fellow Arabs and Jews alike must receive unqualified

The Rejection of Palestinian Self-Determination

condemnation." The resort by some Arabs to the tactic of terrorism was rightly condemned, but the fact that their "fear" and "apprehension" was quite reasonable and justifiable solicited no further comment.

Moreover, the document stated prophetically, if these circumstances continued and Jewish immigration continued to contribute to Arab fears and apprehensions, provoking resistance, "a fatal enmity between the two peoples will be perpetuated, and the situation in Palestine may become a permanent source of friction amongst all peoples in the Near and Middle East." The British government thus perceived that it had a difficult choice to make:

> The alternatives before His Majesty's Government are either (i) to seek to expand the Jewish National Home indefinitely by immigration, against the strongly expressed will of the Arab people of the country; or (ii) to permit further expansion of the Jewish National Home by immigration only if the Arabs are prepared to acquiesce in it. The former policy means rule by force.

In addition, policy option (i) would be contrary to the spirit of the League of Nations and to the British government's "obligations to the Arabs in the Palestine Mandate." Britain, had therefore "decided that the time has come to adopt in principle the second of the alternatives referred to above."

But this statement did not come without qualifications. Britain could not accept the cessation of immigration into Palestine, not only because of its commitments to Zionist leaders in favoring the creation of a Jewish "National Home", but also because the government was "conscious of the present unhappy plight of large numbers of Jews" who were the victims of European anti-Semitism. Palestine, they declared, "can and should make a further contribution to the solution of this pressing world problem." As with the Peel Commission report, no comment was offered as to why the Arabs should be required to further contribute to the solution of the plight of European Jews at the hands of European powers when European countries were not willing to make any similar contribution or an equal "sacrifice".

Thus, it was not policy option (ii), but something much closer to option (i) that Britain would implement, with perhaps the only requisite change in wording being the removal of "indefinitely" from the sentence.

Of course, as acknowledged, this meant "rule by force" contrary to both the spirit of the British Mandate under the League of Nations and to Britain's acknowledged "obligations to the Arabs", and was a decision that would also predictably result in "a fatal enmity" and "a permanent source of friction" in the Middle East. But no matter, the best interests of the Arab Palestinians were what Britain declared them to be. Never mind what Arabs perceived to be their own best interests; they were, after all, under British "tutelage". The White Paper therefore declared, contrary to its own call for representative government, what the *British* had "best calculated to serve the interests of the whole people of Palestine". This would include allowing the continued growth of the Jewish population "up to approximately one third of the total population of the country", which amounted to "some 75,000 immigrants over the next five years". An additional 25,000 refugees would be admitted "as a contribution towards the solution of the Jewish refugee problem". Once this had all been accomplished, the British would regard its obligations to the Zionist leaders as having been fulfilled.

To reiterate, policy option (ii) would be implemented within a framework not dissimilar to Weizmann's own interpretation of "the democratic principle", and would therefore actually more closely resemble option (i).

One might be tempted to accuse the British of being totally inconsistent and self-contradictory, but the matter needs to be understood within this racist colonial framework and its corollary that the British, to borrow from Balfour, "do not propose even to go through the form of consulting the wishes of the present inhabitants of the country". Thus the authors of British policy could plead ignorance as to the true will of the Palestinian majority and, regardless, would simply declare to the Arabs what was good for them anyways, with the expectation that they must accept British "tutelage". Although the true wishes of most of Palestine's inhabitants could not possibly have been unknown to the British, nevertheless, understood within this framework, one can fairly say that the British were not entirely incapable of consistency.

The White Paper also offered some insight into the British view, as expressed by Balfour, about the "present needs" and "future hopes" of Palestine that were "of far profounder import" than Arab self-determination. It observed that nothing had changed since the Peel Commission in that the "sole limiting factor" of Jewish immigration remained the "economic absorptive capacity of the country", despite the recommendation, ignored by those who made it, that other factors should also be considered. This "sole limiting factor" had been "laid down as a matter of policy" in a letter "sent to Dr. Weizmann in February

The Rejection of Palestinian Self-Determination

1931". Again, the views of the majority Arab population were of precisely zero consideration. It was only if "immigration has an adverse effect on the economic position in the country" that "it should clearly be restricted."

This rejection of their rights does not mean that the Arabs did not factor at all into the equation, for their "fear of indefinite Jewish immigration" was so "widespread amongst the Arab population" that it had "made possible disturbances which have given a serious setback to economic progress". In other words, while efforts by the Arabs to resolve the conflict peacefully through negotiation, advancement of democratic principles, and mutual recognition of equal rights proved totally ineffectual, the resort to violence and terrorism at least had the effect of hindering "economic progress" and in that sense had at least in some small measure been successful in achieving its aim. That terrorism worked to some extent where nonviolent means failed utterly was a lesson from British "tutelage" that neither the Arabs nor the Jews were remiss to learn.

That aside, the stated British concern over the plight of Jews in Europe deserves further consideration. Although the Holocaust was yet to come, by 1939 the plight of the Jews in Germany and Poland was hardly unknown to the outside world, and anti-Semitism was prevalent elsewhere in Europe as well.[53] The British government can certainly not be faulted for wanting to assist and accommodate Jews who had sought refuge from European persecution. But neither can one fault the Palestinians for not being willing while under occupation to simply surrender to demands of the occupying power and acquiesce to the redefining through immigration of the geopolitical landscape (a "re-constituted" Palestine, to borrow from Rothschild) on account of prejudices and crimes committed against those immigrants by other European powers. One may criticize the Arabs for not willingly offering up their homeland out of consideration for the plight of the Jews in Europe, but not without hypocrisy. The British, after all, hadn't offered to facilitate the immigration of Jews to England and there to establish a "Jewish National Home" within Great Britain. Nor was any such "sacrifice" imposed upon any other European nation, or the U.S., for that matter.

British policy had set the region on a course for conflict, a fact acknowledged by its designers. The trick for Britain now was to extract itself from the predicament it had created, and to wash its hands of the whole affair.

THE ARAB AND AMERICAN POSITIONS

In 1944, Egypt, Iraq, Jordan, Syria, and Lebanon agreed to establish a joint organization that would result in the formation of the League of Arab States the following year. In an agreement that became known as the Alexandria Protocol, the Arab states declared that "Palestine constitutes an important part of the Arab World and that the rights of the Arabs in Palestine cannot be touched without prejudice to peace and stability in the Arab World." The cessation of Jewish immigration and recognition of the rights of the Arabs would be a step towards the goal of "the stabilization of peace and security." While announcing support for the rights of the Arab Palestinians, the Arab Committee also declared

> that it is second to none in regretting the woes which have been inflicted upon the Jews of Europe by European dictatorial states. But the

The Rejection of Palestinian Self-Determination

question of these Jews should not be confused with Zionism, for there can be no greater injustice and aggression than solving the problem of the Jews of Europe by another injustice".⁵⁴

In the founding document of the Arab League, its member nations agreed that any instance of aggression or the threat of aggression would be referred immediately to the Council of the League of Arab States for a decision on what action would be taken in response. The pact declared that with the end of the First World War, Palestine "became independent, not belonging to any other States" and that its fate "should be decided by the parties concerned in Palestine."⁵⁵

The U.S. policy towards Palestine, meanwhile, while still ambiguous, was evolving towards favoring the Zionist project. By 1922, support for Zionism had grown in the U.S. to the extent that the Congress passed a joint resolution parroting the Balfour Declaration in stating that

> the United States of America favors the establishment in Palestine of a national home for the Jewish people, it being clearly understood that nothing shall be done which may prejudice the civil and religious rights of Christian and all other non-Jewish communities in Palestine, and that the Holy places and religious buildings and sites in Palestine shall be adequately protected.⁵⁶

On March 16, 1945, President Franklin D. Roosevelt authorized a public statement made by Rabbi Stephen S. Wise, head of the Zionist Organization of America, that he supported unlimited Jewish immigration to Palestine and the establishment of a Jewish state. But then on April 6, Roosevelt issued a letter to King Abdul Aziz ibn Saud of Saudi Arabia that expressed "the attitude of the American Government toward Palestine". It was the "desire" of the U.S. "that no decision be taken with respect to the basic situation in that country without full consultation with both Arabs and Jews."[57]

Whatever Roosevelt's intended meaning had been, the interpretation of "full consultation" under his successor President Harry S. Truman would become apparent. On November 10, 1945, President Truman met with U.S. diplomats posted in the Middle East, who urged him against supporting the Zionist aspiration that, in the words of Lord Rothschild, "Palestine should be re-constituted as the National Home for the Jewish People." Truman responded by explaining his reason for supporting this goal: "I'm sorry, gentlemen, but I have to answer to hundreds of thousands who are anxious for the success of Zionism: I do not have hundreds of thousands of Arabs among my constituents."[58]

THE ANGLO-AMERICAN COMMITTEE OF INQUIRY

In 1946, Britain and the U.S. led a joint inquiry in an attempt to assess the situation in order to implement a unified policy. The Anglo-American Committee of Inquiry report stated that "Palestine alone cannot meet the emigration needs of the Jewish victims of Nazi and Fascist persecution; the whole world shares responsibility for them and indeed for the resettlement of all 'displaced persons'". Laws and restrictions then in place barred the entry of Jewish refugees and European countries should make at least temporary special provisions in their existing immigration laws to accommodate refugees. However, the report said, "much time must pass before such laws and restrictions can be altered", with no explanation as to why changes to immigration policy to accommodate Jewish refugees could not be made effective immediately.

Instead, for "the immediate future", Jews should go to Palestine, "where almost all of them want to go" anyways. In Palestine, Jews would "receive a welcome denied them elsewhere" from a minority of the population. "Elsewhere" presumably included European countries, where, if we draw the obvious corollary, there was not even a minority who would welcome the Jews. This might in turn help to explain why "much time must pass" before European countries would extend a helping hand while Arab Palestinians were forced to "sacrifice" immediately as a solution to the problem.

Immigration, the report recommended, should continue, with 100,000 certificates of immigration to be "authorized immediately" (notice that "much time" need not pass for Palestine to be able to accept refugees, only for European countries to do so). Additionally, the report recommended that "actual immigration be pushed forward as rapidly as conditions will permit", presumably meaning as much as the "economic absorptive capacity" of Palestine would allow. "Receiving so large a number", the report admitted, "will be a heavy burden on Palestine." But that was a matter of very little concern.

Under Truman's interpretation of Roosevelt's principle of "full consultation", the Arabs had been consulted by the committee; their views and concerns were summarily dismissed. Of those "who have opposed the admission of these unfortunate people into Palestine", the report remarked, "if they cannot see their way to help, at least they will not make the position of these sufferers more difficult." The report had no similar lecture for European countries that must be allowed "much time" before sharing the "heavy burden". The Arabs must simply accept that they have to "sacrifice", to borrow from the Peel Commission report, and they were expected to not put up a fuss about it.

The commission's report determined that neither people should dominate the other and declared that "Palestine shall be neither a Jewish state nor an Arab state", while implementing a policy that rejected representative government, rejected the Arab position, and assisted the Zionists in furthering their stated goal of establishing a Jewish state and thus dominating the Arabs. Palestine's "Arab population, descended from long-time inhabitants of the area, rightly look upon Palestine as their homeland", but "The Jewish National Home, though embodying a minority of the population, is today a reality established under international guarantee. It has a right to continued existence, protection *and development*" (emphasis added).

Continuing, the report observed that "any form of constitution in which a mere numerical majority is decisive" would be insufficient, and the democratic option was thus rejected. The committee might have noted the fact that the U.S. Constitution contains measures to protect the rights of the minority so that "numerical majority" alone was not the sole deciding factor in government. They might also have noted that the Arabs proposed something that would mirror this model and guarantee minority rights. But these fairly elementary observations seemed somehow to escape the American and British members of the committee. Their report did briefly mention the possibility of "minority guarantees" but then dismissed the idea offhand as inadequate, without explanation or further comment. We are left to speculate as to their reasons

The Rejection of Palestinian Self-Determination

for this, but one contributing factor was no doubt an awareness of the fact that any such proposal would have been met with rejection from Zionist leaders, who could help assure that Palestine would become an "outpost of civilization" holding off the "barbarism" of the east.

Representative democracy was out. As for partition, it "would result in civil strife such as might threaten the peace of the world". So that was out, too. The conclusion of the committee, therefore, was that Palestine should remain under foreign occupation until a "trusteeship agreement" could be established under the United Nations. The Palestine question, in other words, would continue to be put off in favor of the status quo and the continuation of existing policies that rejected any democratic solution and which were well recognized by both the British and American governments to be leading down the road towards catastrophe.

It is difficult to say whether the report reflected the sheer incompetence or the outright duplicity of the committee. Either way, the report continued to contradict itself at every turn. To cite several further examples, it stated that neither Arabs nor Jews should have a majority and thus "control the destiny" of the other, but the obvious and absurd corollary that Jewish immigration should therefore continue until there were precisely an equal number of Jews as Arabs passed without comment. It stated that the rights and position of the Arabs should not be prejudiced, but then rejected "the view that there shall be no further Jewish immigration into Palestine without Arab acquiescence". It declared rejection of "the insistent Jewish demand that forced Jewish immigration must proceed apace" to further the goal of a Jewish state, while at the same time refusing to limit immigration, recommending that immigration be "pushed forward as rapidly as conditions will permit", and recommending the rescinding of restrictions on Jewish land purchases designed for "preventing the creation of a considerable landless Arab population". Further examples of the committee's cognitive dissonance abound, but it would be superfluous to list them further.

The report did, however, mention a few other noteworthy facts. It noted Palestine's geographic and "strategic importance", and that it is "deeply involved in the business and politics of the international trade in oil" with a pipeline to refineries at the port of Haifa. A U.S. arrangement with the Saudi kingdom might mean a second pipeline there, as well.

The population of Palestine by the end of 1944 had reached 1,765,000, with the Jewish population rising from 84,000 in 1922 to 554,000, or nearly one-third of the whole. The increase in the Jewish population was mostly due to immigration while that of the Arabs was due to natural increase. Some Jews in the U.S. and Britain joined "important sections of Middle Eastern Jewry" in opposing Zionism.

The report also stated that "Jews in Palestine are convinced that Arab violence paid" (recall the lesson of British "tutelage" discussed previously). The Jewish view was accompanied by the Anglo-American one that one "immediate result of the success of Arab terrorism was the beginning of Jewish terrorism". The Mandatory Government was "not only condemned verbally, but attacked with bombs and firearms by organized bands of Jewish terrorists." Gangs of terrorists were increasing in strength and enjoyed "widespread popular support" among Jews. The "National Home" was becoming increasingly militaristic. "A sinister aspect of recent years is the development of large illegal armed forces", namely, the Haganah. The Irgun Zvai Leumi was a splinter group of the Haganah that had been formed in 1935. In turn, the Stern Gang had splintered from the Irgun and was likewise responsible for acts of terrorism.

The report's remarks on the position of the Arabs are also instructive. It observed that their view was "based upon the fact that Palestine is a country which the Arabs have occupied for more than a thousand years" and that by issuing the Balfour Declaration, "the British Government were [sic] giving away something that did not belong to Britain". The British Mandate itself "conflicted with the Covenant of the League of Nations" and was "a violation of their right to self-determination since it is forcing upon them an immigration which they do not desire and will not tolerate—an invasion of Palestine by the Jews." Moreover, "The suggestion that self-government should be withheld from Palestine until the Jews have acquired a majority seems outrageous to the Arabs." Each of these views, though correct, was rejected implicitly if not explicitly by the committee. Rejection of Arab self-determination was by no means "outrageous" to the British.

Continuing, the committee commented that Arab objections were not based on anti-Semitism, and "indeed, they are Semites themselves." Rather, Arabs professed

> the greatest sympathy for the persecuted Jews of Europe, but they point out that they have not been responsible for this persecution and that it is not just that they should be compelled to atone for the sins of Western peoples by accepting into their country hundreds of thousands of victims of European anti-Semitism.

The Rejection of Palestinian Self-Determination

Some of the Arab representatives even expressed a willingness to provide for Jewish refugees on a quota basis if the U.S., Britain, and other Western countries would do the same. But following the convention of British "tutelage", the commission instead insisted that Jewish immigration was good for the Arabs even though "they prefer freedom." Arab "exasperation at the disregard" of the British position had been the cause of earlier revolts. Arabs throughout Palestine and neighboring countries, including Muslims and Christians, were in solidarity in opposing the "invasion" of their homeland.

The commission candidly stated, "It is not surprising that the Arabs have bitterly resented this invasion and have resisted it by force of arms." Their report then went on to explain that this is because the Arab Palestinians are so backwards. Applying Weizmann's "democratic principle", their views may thus be dismissed and their rights unrecognized, which is precisely what the committee did in its recommendations.[59]

Following the release of the report, President Truman implemented some of its recommendations as policy, issuing a statement on October 4 noting that he had urged that immediate steps be taken to relieve their plight by "admitting 100,000 Jews", not into the U.S., but "into Palestine" (it being then, as now, simply a matter of faith—an assumption that regularly passes without comment—that the U.S. has the authority to declare policy on behalf of other people in other lands). The statement also noted that the Jewish Agency had proposed the creation of a Jewish state in Palestine that would be allowed to control its own immigration. This "solution", Truman declared, without evidence, would be supported by American public opinion.[60] The public opinion of the majority in Palestine, once again, though well known, was of zero consideration.

IV. THE U.N. PARTITION PLAN AND ARAB 'CATASTROPHE'

In 1947, Great Britain, unable to reconcile its conflicting obligations to both Jews and Arabs, requested that the United Nations take up the question of Palestine. In May, the U.N. Special Committee on Palestine (UNSCOP) was created by a General Assembly resolution. UNSCOP's purpose was to investigate the situation in Palestine and "submit such proposals as it may consider appropriate for the solution of the problem of Palestine". At the time, the U.N. consisted of 55 members, including Egypt, Iraq, Lebanon, and Syria. Palestine by then remained the only one of the formerly Mandated Territories not to become an independent state. No representatives from any Arab nations, however, were included in UNSCOP. [61] Egypt, Iraq, Syria, Lebanon, and Saudi Arabia requested that "The termination of the Mandate over Palestine and the declaration of its independence" be placed on the agenda, but this motion was rejected. The Arab Higher Committee thus announced it would not collaborate, although individual Arab states did agree to meet with representatives from UNSCOP.[62]

UNSCOP's investigation included a 15-day tour of Palestine, splitting time between visits to Arab and Jewish communities. Seven days—nearly half that same amount of time spent touring Palestine itself—were spent touring Displaced Persons (D.P.) camps in Germany and Austria and witnessing the plight of the Jews there.[63] The proposal to visit the D.P. camps passed by a vote of six to four with one abstention, despite the objection from two members that it would be "improper to connect the displaced persons, and the Jewish problem as a whole, with the problem of Palestine".[64] More time was spent visiting D.P. camps than the total number of days spent visiting the Arab nations neighboring Palestine and meeting with representatives there. Public hearings were held in which 37 representatives were heard, 31 of whom were Jews representing 17 Jewish organizations, but with only one representative from each of the six Arab states.[65] Two proposals emerged: a federal State plan and a partition plan. The latter passed by a vote of seven to three with one abstention, the dissenting votes being cast by India, Iran, and Yugoslavia, who all favored the federal state plan.

On September 3, UNSCOP submitted its report to the U.N. General Assembly. The report noted that the population of Palestine at the end of 1946 was estimated to be almost 1,846,000, with 1,203,000 Arabs (65 percent) and 608,000 Jews (33 percent). Again, the growth of the Jewish population was mainly the result of immigration, whereas the Arab growth was "almost entirely" natural increase. Complicating any notion of partition, UNSCOP observed that there was "no clear territorial separation of Jews and Arabs by large contiguous areas." In the Jaffa district, for example, which included Tel Aviv, "Jews are more than 40 per cent of the total population", with an Arab majority.[66]

Land ownership statistics from 1945 showed that Arabs owned more land than Jews in every single district in Palestine. In Jaffa, with the highest percentage of Jewish ownership of any district, 47 percent of the land was owned by Arabs versus 39 percent owned by Jews. At the opposite end of the spectrum, in

The Rejection of Palestinian Self-Determination

Ramallah district, Arabs owned 99 percent of the land and Jews less than 1 percent.[67] In the whole of Palestine, Arabs were in possession of 85 percent of the land, while Jews owned less than 7 percent.[68]

UNSCOP mentioned in its report that Jewish groups such as the Irgun and the Stern Gang had engaged in terrorism, including the bombing of the King David Hotel. While Jewish leaders had "from time to time condemned terrorist activities, and there have been some signs of active opposition to such methods on the part of the Haganah", terrorism was a widely enough accepted tactic among the Zionists that the British had "found it necessary to arrest and detain on grounds of public security some 2,600 Jews, including four members of the Jewish Agency Executive." UNSCOP also related the characterization from the British Administration in Palestine that "Since the beginning of 1945 the Jews have . . . supported by an organized campaign of lawlessness, murder and sabotage their contention that . . . nothing should be allowed to stand in the way of a Jewish State and free Jewish immigration into Palestine."

During one of its hearings, the Arab representatives expressed their view with regard to the Zionist "recourse to terrorism", which was that "This aggressive attitude . . . will not fail to give rise in turn to the creation of similar [terrorist] organizations by the Arabs." The Arab delegates also declared that "against a [Jewish] State established by violence, the Arab States will be obliged to use violence; that is a legitimate right of self-defence."

The case of the Zionist Jews, UNSCOP reported, was based on biblical arguments as well as on the Balfour Declaration, which, they contended, recognized their "right" to colonize

50

The Rejection of Palestinian Self-Determination

Palestine. Their case also rested on the false claim that "immigrant Jews displace no Arabs" and upon the assertion that the establishment of a Jewish State would "do no political injustice to the Arabs, since the Arabs have never established a government in Palestine." In other words, the Arab right to self-determination could be denied now because that right had never been recognized or exercised in the past (logic which would prove problematic for democracies everywhere, but the delight of kings and tyrants, if the standard were actually applied to other cases).

The Zionists also argued that once a Jewish State is established and the Jews become a majority, the Arab minority "will be fully protected in all its rights on an equal basis with the Jewish citizenry." This was not accompanied with any explanation as to why this should be acceptable to the then Arab majority, or why the Arabs should accept what the Zionists themselves had rejected.

The entire Zionist case was outrageous. Its arguments were spurious, prejudiced and hypocritical to the extreme. And yet UNSCOP took them quite seriously. It accepted without question the assumption that the British had the right to open Palestine for colonization while it was under occupation, an action that would be expressly forbidden under the Geneva Conventions just two years later.[69] It accepted the argument that to allow democracy in Palestine "would in fact destroy the Jewish National Home" and on that basis explicitly rejected the right to self-determination of the Arab majority. It mentioned in passing that the Balfour Declaration had a clause stating that nothing should be done to prejudice the rights and positions of the Arab majority, commenting only that the guarantee of "civil and religious" rights excluded "political" rights and thus did not

The Rejection of Palestinian Self-Determination

translate into a promise of "political freedom to the Arab population of Palestine".

UNSCOP also observed that the use of the term "National Home" instead of "State" "had the advantage of not shocking public opinion outside the Jewish world", which is precisely why it was chosen. Furthermore, echoing the McDonald White Paper, it also asserted that the use of this term did not preclude the possibility of establishing a Jewish State; a statement that could only be maintained by prejudicing position and rights of the Arabs.

UNSCOP also effectively accepted the biblical argument, reiterating that the 1922 White Paper had recognized the "ancient historic connection" of the Jews to Palestine and accepting this as giving Jews from Europe and elsewhere the "right" to colonize the occupied territory. (Compare this with the conclusion of the King-Crane Commission that the claim that Jews "have a 'right' to Palestine, based on an occupation of 2,000 years ago, can hardly be seriously considered.") It recognized the corollary "that all Jews in the world who wish to go to Palestine would have the right to do so." But its only reservation about this conclusion was that it "would seem to be unrealistic in the sense that a country as small and poor as Palestine could never accommodate all the Jews in the world." Again, the rights and position of the Arab majority simply did not factor into the equation.

Astonishingly, while UNSCOP observed that "all concerned were aware of the existence of an overwhelming Arab majority", that "the Zionist program could not be carried out except by force of arms", and that "the basic assumption" was that the Arabs would acquiesce quietly, the committee's only comment about any of this was that the assumption of Arab acquiescence "proved to be a false one".

Other assumptions adopted by UNSCOP were equally astonishing. As yet a further example, it partially accepted the argument that "no political injustice would be done to the Arabs by the creation of a Jewish State in Palestine" because "not since 63 B.C., when Pompey stormed Jerusalem, has Palestine been an independent State." This logic reflected the committee's acceptance of the Zionists' ludicrous argument that since the Arab Palestinians had not exercised self-determination in the past, therefore this right could continue to be denied them into the future. Or take UNSCOP's assertion that the solution required "the postponement of independence" until "the Jewish people become a majority" in the part of the country dedicated against the will of the Arab majority to the "Jewish National Home". In sum, the U.N. Special Committee on Palestine operated under assumptions that explicitly rejected the rights of the Arabs.

Having already accepted a rejectionist framework, the UNSCOP report then proceeded to examine the Arab position. Its examination is further instructive as to the absolutely prejudicial nature of the committee. It asserted that the Arabs, for instance, only "postulate" that they have majority rights since "they are and have been for many centuries in possession of the land", uninterrupted since "early historical times". But, as already noted, the committee denied that Arabs had majority rights with the adoption of the Zionist argument that "they have not been in possession of it as a sovereign nation".

The Arabs merely "claim" that "general promises and pledges officially made to the Arab people in the course of the First World War" recognized their rights and supported an

The Rejection of Palestinian Self-Determination

independent Palestine. But this is just their "view", not a fact; the committee held that "apparently there is no unequivocal agreement as to whether Palestine was included within the territory pledged" and "Great Britain has consistently denied that Palestine was among the territories to which independence was pledged." In other words, since the British had rejected the rights of the Arab Palestinians, UNSCOP would also do so.

The Arabs only "allege" that the Mandate violated the Covenant of the League of Nations which prescribed that Mandate territories become independent. Here, UNSCOP actually made a reasonably strong case. The relevant article of the Covenant, they pointed out, merely discussed independence as being "permissible", not obligatory. Moreover, the Allied Powers had accepted the policy of the Balfour Declaration, making it "clear from the beginning that Palestine would have been treated differently from Syria and Iraq" in that, in Palestine, the right to self-determination of the Arabs would be denied. There would therefore "seem to be no grounds for questioning the validity of the Mandate for the reason advanced by the Arab States." And UNSCOP came up with none of its own reasons for doing so.

In a particularly remarkable illustration of UNSCOP's prejudice, it implored people to remember that, as Lord Balfour had explained at the creation of the Mandate, "a mandate is a self-imposed limitation by the conquerors on the sovereignty which they obtained over conquered territories" according not to the will of the inhabitants, but to what the occupiers "conceived to be the general welfare of mankind".[70] In other words, self-determination was not an inherent right, but a privilege granted to a territory's inhabitants by their conquerors should the occupying power at its own discretion choose to

The Rejection of Palestinian Self-Determination

bestow the gift upon them. An occupied people were not to decide for themselves what is in their best interests; this was to be dictated to them by the foreign power occupying their land. This framework was accepted matter-of-factly by UNSCOP, despite being in direct contradiction to the principles of the U.N. Charter under which it was commissioned. In fact, just three years later, the International Court of Justice would rule that the creation of a Mandate under the Covenant of the League of Nations "did not involve any cession of territory or transfer of sovereignty".[71]

UNSCOP offered only the slightest pretense that its findings were anything but rejectionist, finding some occasion to pay lip-service to the principles of equal rights and self-determination. It asserted, for instance, that Britain was "not free to dispose of Palestine without regard for the wishes and interests of the inhabitants of Palestine" while itself proposing to do just that (presumably, in their view, it took the higher authority of first the League of Nations and then the U.N. to dispose of Palestine against the will of its inhabitants).

In their report, the committee acknowledged candidly that under the Mandate "the principle of self-determination . . . was not applied to Palestine, obviously because of the intention to make possible the creation of the Jewish National Home there", which, along with the Mandate itself, was recognized to be "counter to that principle" of democracy (presumably also "obviously" so).

UNSCOP acknowledged that if the right to self-determination of the Arabs was respected, they "would recognize the right of Jews to continue in possession of land legally acquired by them during the Mandate", as they had offered at the London conference and again proposed to UNSCOP. But the point was moot since their rights "obviously" were not recognized.

Having established this rejectionist framework, UNSCOP proceeded to weigh the proposed solutions, which included partition, a unitary state, or a single state "with a federal, cantonal or binational structure". Most Jewish organizations consulted wanted a Jewish State, with different views as to whether this state should constitute the whole of Palestine or only a part. But some among those consulted were opposed to the Zionist program, including in the U.S. the American Council for Judaism, which viewed any partition plan as a threat to peace, harmful to Jews, and undemocratic.

As noted, the Arab representatives reiterated something similar to what had been proposed at the conference in London a year earlier: a unitary Palestine with a democratic constitution guaranteeing full civil and religious rights for all citizens and an elected legislative assembly that would include Jewish representatives. UNSCOP dismissed this as "an extreme position". In accordance with their adopted framework, the Arab proposal for a single democratic state was rejected as "extreme" because it didn't take into account the desires of the Zionists, who rejected the idea. And yet the partition recommendation was not similarly "extreme" despite being "strongly opposed by Arabs". The federal state solution, moreover, was simply "unworkable", UNSCOP asserted in its majority recommendation, without discussion.

India, Iran, and Yugoslavia dissented, arguing that the federal state solution was "in every respect the most democratic solution" and "most in harmony with the basic principles of the Charter of the United Nations". It was supported by "a substantial number of Jews", whereas the partition plan was

The Rejection of Palestinian Self-Determination

supported by no Arabs, and was the solution that would therefore "best serve the interests of both Arabs and Jews."

The dissenting view aside, UNSCOP's final recommendation was that the Mandate be terminated and independence "granted" to Palestine, with the caveat that there was "vigorous disagreement as to the form that independence should take." Partition was recommended since the "claims to Palestine of the Arabs and Jews, both possessing equal validity, are irreconcilable", the assumption being that because Jews had "historic roots" there, a Jew from Europe who had never set foot in Palestine had an equal right to the land as an Arab whose family had lived and worked there for generations. The "demerit of the scheme" was that while there would be "an insignificant minority of Jews" in the proposed Arab State, "in the Jewish State there will be a considerable minority of Arabs." But this was "inevitable" since the democratic solution was to be rejected.[72]

On October 11, 1947, a U.S. representative to the United Nations expressed the U.S. policy position of supporting the partition of Palestine to facilitate the creation of a Jewish state.[73]

The U.N. General Assembly on November 29 passed Resolution 181, recommending that UNSCOP's partition plan be implemented. The resolution called upon "the inhabitants of Palestine to take such steps as may be necessary on their part to put this plan into effect".[74]

One enduring myth about the Israeli-Palestinian conflict is that "Israel was created by the U.N." under General Assembly Resolution 181.[75] This claim is absolutely false. While the General Assembly is the more democratic of the two U.N. bodies, only Security Council resolutions are considered legally binding. Resolution 181 was nothing more than a recommendation. Naturally, any such plan would have to be acceptable to both parties, and it was not. The plan would have awarded a majority of the territory to its minority Jewish population, who were in possession of a mere fraction of the land, and so was naturally rejected by the Arab majority who legally owned most of Palestine.[76] Regardless, the U.N. was no more "free to dispose of Palestine without regard for the wishes and interests of the inhabitants of Palestine" than Great Britain, and any U.N. resolution from either body that would have sought to do so would have been a violation of the U.N.'s own Charter and therefore null and void.

ZIONIST TERRORISM

As noted earlier, neither the Arabs nor the Jews were remiss to learn the lesson under British "tutelage" that terrorism may succeed where non-violent efforts fail. Among the Zionists were some factions who employed the tactic against Arabs and the British alike.

Today the very word "Palestinian" is often invoked as being virtually synonymous with "terrorist". Palestinian violence is constantly pinpointed as the root cause of the continuing conflict, rather than a consequence of the rejection of Arab self-determination. This narrative is well known, and repeated *ad nauseam*, with examples being too numerous to mention. Yet the role early in the conflict's history of Jews engaging in terrorism is regularly omitted from accounts purporting to identify root causes, and it therefore warrants a brief emphasis.

To cite just a few examples, on November 6, 1944, the British Colonial Secretary Lord Moyne was assassinated in

The Rejection of Palestinian Self-Determination

Cairo by terrorists from the *Lohamei Herut Israel* (Fighters for the Freedom of Israel), known more commonly by the Hebrew acronym Lehi, or simply as the Stern Gang after the group's founder, Avraham Stern.[77] One notable member of Lehi was Yitzhak Shamir, who would go on to become Prime Minister of Israel in 1986.[78]

On July 22, 1946, the Irgun was responsible for bombing the King David Hotel in Jerusalem, which contained the offices of the Government Secretariat and part of military headquarters, killing 91 people. 86 of the victims were public servants. 41 Arabs, 28 Britons, and 17 Jews were murdered.[79] The commander of the Irgun at the time was Menachem Begin, who would go on to be elected Prime Minister of Israel in 1977.[80]

A British contemporary account noted that "Later terrorist activities have included the kidnapping of a British judge and of British officers, sabotage of the railway system and of oil installations at Haifa, and the blowing up of a British Officers' Club in Jerusalem with considerable loss of life."[81]

According to another British report, the Haganah was engaged in "planned movements of sabotage and violence under the guise of 'the Jewish Resistance Movement'". On certain operations, the Haganah worked with the Irgun and the Stern Gang, groups supported by the radio station "Kol Israel", which was "under the general direction of the Jewish Agency".[82]

On January 4, 1948, Irgun terrorists detonated a truck bomb in the city of Jaffa, killing 26 and wounding 100 Palestinians, including women and children.[83]

Lehi was responsible for the assassination of Count Folke Bernadotte of Sweden in Jerusalem on September 17, 1948.[84]

The Rejection of Palestinian Self-Determination

On April 9, 1948, members from both Lehi and the Irgun took part in a massacre at the Arab village of Deir Yasin, where 254 men, women, and children were murdered.[85]

These examples, by no means an exhaustive list, serve to demonstrate that the Arabs are not alone in resorting to violence in an attempt to achieve political ends, contrary to the standard narrative wherein Israelis are invariably the innocent victims of Palestinian terrorism—but never vice versa.

THE BIRTH OF A NATION

The rejection of Arab self-determination predates the creation of the state of Israel, and was manifest in the Zionist goal of establishing *Eretz Israel* in all of Palestine, in the duplicitous and racist British colonialist policies, in the policy position eventually taken by the U.S. that mirrored that of Great Britain, in the framework adopted by the U.N. Special Commission on Palestine, and in the resultant General Assembly resolution recommending partition.

But recognition of the rejectionist nature of the framework adopted in deciding the fate of Palestine is a mere first step. Further consequences should be considered in light of the basis of policies implemented under that framework. In particular, it would be remiss for us not to at least briefly discuss the most immediate and significant manifestation of this prejudicial framework: the birth of the state of Israel.

On May 14, 1948, the Zionist leadership under David Ben-Gurion declared the establishment of the state of Israel. The U.S. announced recognition of Israel immediately, and other nations followed, while the neighboring Arab states took up arms in an attempt to prevent the forceful annexation of

Palestinian territory and further atrocities against its Arab inhabitants.

Significantly, no borders for the newly proclaimed state were specified, while the founding declaration document made reference to *Eretz Israel* and cited the Old Testament ("the eternal Book of Books") as the foundation for its legitimacy, implying that the newly declared state included *all* of Palestine. The document also made reference to the Balfour Declaration and its reaffirmation under the Palestine Mandate of the League of Nations as a further claim to legitimacy. Additionally, it cited U.N. General Assembly Resolution 181 as "recognition by the United Nations of the right of the Jewish people to establish their State", which was "irrevocable". It stated that "every Jew", anywhere in the world, had a right to immigrate and resettle in Palestine.[86]

There's no shortage of literary and academic work on the subject of Israel's creation. Much work has been done, including by prominent Israeli scholars and historians, documenting events of this period, including the ethnic cleansing of Palestine. To Jews, there was a "War of Independence". To Arabs, there was the "Nakba" or "Catastrophe". Both describe the same events. The purpose here is to merely provide a brief overview of what occurred, and for that we can turn to a fairly recent example, from the journal *Foreign Affairs*, in which Shlomo Ben-Ami provides a summary account of these events.

This article has been chosen as a useful overview for several reasons. First, *Foreign Affairs* is a preeminent and well-respected journal upon which is generally conferred a great deal of credibility. Second, the author is a notable Israeli and former Foreign Minister, so it's reasonable to presume that if there is bias in it, it's in favor of Israel and against the Arabs.

The Rejection of Palestinian Self-Determination

Conclusions and opinions aside, we may presume that the facts he presents are non-controversial, and we may eliminate the charge of anti-Israeli bias that might otherwise be made against another author writing the exact same things. Third, the above presumptions apply not only to the author, but also to his primary source, also Israeli. Fourth, the article not only offers insights not only into the past framework, but demonstrates how it continues today.

The article to is entitled "A War to Start All Wars: Will Israel Ever Seal the Victory of 1948?" from the September/October 2008 issue of *Foreign Affairs*.[87] The title itself offers a bit of insight, as it implicitly acknowledges that the continuing conflict is rooted in the war of 1948. Its description of events that occurred as then as constituting a "victory" offers a clue about the point of view of the writer.

Ben-Ami begins by observing that nations often mythologize their own histories to "confer legitimacy" upon themselves, when the truth is that "Throughout history, nations have been born in blood and frequently in sin." Zionists "were not the first" to so embellish their accounts. Of the Zionist "myth", he explains that, "To the Israelis, the 1948 war was a desperate fight for survival". At the same time, he asserts that "the noble Jewish dream of statehood was stained by the sins of Israel's birth".

Historians more recently have challenged "the Zionist mythology surrounding Israel's birth", the "conventional view of the war as a clash between a Jewish David and an Arab Goliath." Among these historians is Benny Morris, who tackled the "most sensitive issue of all: the refugee crisis", in his book *The Birth of the Palestinian Refugee Problem, 1947-1949*, which "recounts the often violent expulsion of 700,000 Arabs as

The Rejection of Palestinian Self-Determination

Jewish soldiers conquered villages and towns throughout Palestine."

Ben-Ami, offering a clue as to the point of view of his source, notes that "Morris famously lamented that the architects of Israel's 1948 war strategy had not more thoroughly purged the Jewish state of its Arab population."

Among the other myths Morris dispels is "the notion of Israel's 'purity of arms'", which he accomplishes by turning to "vast numbers of primary sources" documenting that "the Zionists committed more massacres than the Arabs, deliberately killed far more civilians and prisoners of war, and committed more acts of rape."

An "offensive strategy" known as "Plan D" adopted by Ben-Gurion in March 1948—one month before the Deir Yassin massacre and two months before the unilateral declaration of the state of Israel and military intervention by neighboring Arab states—was "a push to extend the frontiers of the future Jewish state beyond the partition lines by linking Jewish population hubs to outlying settlements."

Of the ethnic cleansing that followed, Ben-Ami observes that "Israel's leaders were not blind to the evolving Palestinian tragedy." Ben-Gurion himself had a "profound awareness that a monumental disaster had befallen the Palestinians" in what Ben-Ami terms "The Palestinian Exodus" (with no recognizable parallel to the Hebrew Exodus from Egypt). Some Palestinians, with the terror of Deir Yassin fresh on their minds, fled "for fear of military attacks", but "far more Palestinians were expelled on explicit orders from commanders in the field". "This is not surprising given that the idea of population transfers had a long and solid pedigree in Zionist thought." The ethnic cleansing of Palestine "stemmed from an ideological predisposition in the

The Rejection of Palestinian Self-Determination

Jewish community". Zionist leaders "generally agreed, as Morris points out, on the benefits of 'transfer'—a euphemism for 'expulsion'" (Ben-Ami's own euphemism for "ethnic cleansing").

The acknowledgment that the ethnic cleansing was premeditated might perhaps explain why Israeli leaders "were not blind" to it, as well as Ben-Gurion's own "profound awareness" of the consequences of policies he was largely responsible for setting in motion, but Ben-Ami offers no further comment in that regard.

Ben-Ami makes no effort to challenge the idea of "benefits" for the Jews resulting from the ethnic cleansing, but rather, in an apparent attempt to grant it legitimacy, asserts that "The idea of forced transfer was explicitly endorsed by the British government's 1937 Peel Commission on Palestine, and Jewish forces began to implement it in the storm of battle in 1948." In October, Ben-Gurion—perhaps demonstrating his "profound awareness" of the situation—had declared, "The Arabs of the Land of Israel have only one function left to them—to run away." Observes Ben-Ami:

> And they did; panic-stricken, they fled in the face of massacres in Ein Zeitun and Eilabun, just as they had done in the wake of an earlier massacre in Deir Yassin. Operational orders, such as the instruction from Moshe Carmel, the Israeli commander of the northern front, "to attack in order to conquer, to kill among the men, to destroy and burn the villages," were carved into the collective memory of the Palestinians, spawning hatred and resentment for generations.

The Rejection of Palestinian Self-Determination

"Palestinian refugees were forced into the wilderness of exile", Ben-Ami continues, "with no guarantee of a new national home and no prospect of returning to their native land. The yearning for return thus became the Palestinians' defining national ethos."

Ben-Ami faults Morris' account on only "two points". The first is that "He is unconvincing in his attempt to pardon some of Israel's original sins" (recall Morris' suggestion that Israel should have done a more thorough job of ethnically cleansing Palestine). The second is his "characterization of the conflict of 1948 as an Islamic jihad against Jewish-Western infidels in Palestine", which "is also unpersuasive."

But the ethnic cleansing of Palestine and the brutal means by which it was accomplished is not in dispute. Ben-Ami affirms these basic facts, now uncontroversial.

Continuing, Ben-Ami writes that "Morris' scrupulous research shows how the 1948 expulsion of the Palestinian Arabs was in no small measure driven by a desire for land among Israeli settlers, who grabbed it and then actively pressured the Israeli government to prevent the Arab refugees from returning to their villages."

This is a considerable understatement. Indeed, the very existence of Israel as a "Jewish state" required a Jewish majority, which made land-grabbing and the forced "population transfer" a prerequisite. This, presumably, was a part of the "ideological predisposition" Ben-Ami referred to earlier, the source, no doubt, of Ben-Gurion's "profound awareness".

This "redemption of the land", he adds, in a tacit acknowledgment of the understatement, "was encouraged just as enthusiastically by Labor Zionists as by those on the right" and "was always central to the Zionist enterprise."

The Rejection of Palestinian Self-Determination

Ben-Ami also acknowledges that the idea of "separation" of Jews and Arabs, a "logical goal for the Zionists", was "never natural for the Palestinian national movement. Many Palestinian nationalists wanted an Arab state with a Jewish minority". In other words, they wanted recognition of their right to self-determination. We may recall that they wanted to exercise this right through representative government, including a constitution that would protect the rights of the Jewish minority. But this is "a peaceful paradise lost" that "has never been practical", asserts Ben-Ami, for reasons that are by now familiar, but which Ben-Ami declines to elaborate upon.

While acknowledging Israel's "sins" of the past, they were the means to an end he nevertheless regards as a "victory". The "sins" he refers to presumably include the massacres and rapes. But it's unclear whether he includes the "expulsion" among Israel's "sins" or the whether this is an inseparable part of the "victory" itself, but his attempt to offer legitimacy to the "expulsion" would suggest the latter. In any case, his own paradigm assumes key aspects of the framework of the early Zionists, and in particular its rejection of Arab rights.

V. Conclusion

It was this rejection of Arab rights that led to increasing conflicts between Arab and Jewish communities in Palestine during the British occupation, as acknowledged at the time by the occupiers. Other events were not so much a consequence of this rejection of Arab rights as a manifestation of it. Such manifestations included the rejection of a democratic solution, the unilateral declaration of the establishment of the state of Israel, and the ethnic cleansing of Palestine. These events in turn helped to ensure further conflict.

It might be useful, in closing, to recall the words of Lord Sydenham that "the harm done by dumping down an alien population upon an Arab country . . . may never be remedied", that the Mandate would "start a running sore in the East, and no one can tell how far that sore will extend". Or the prediction of the 1939 White Paper that as a result of British and Zionist policies in Palestine, "a fatal enmity between the two peoples will be perpetuated, and the situation in Palestine may become a permanent source of friction amongst all peoples in the Near and Middle East."

The horrible consequences of the rejection of the right of the Arab Palestinians to self-determination were predictable, and predicted. The further consequences of continuing to deny the Palestinians that right today are no less predictable, and unlikely to be any less tragic. Now, as then, there is a choice.

NOTES

[1] The Sykes-Picot Agreement of 1916, available online at the Yale Avalon Project website: http://avalon.law.yale.edu.
[2] Division for Palestinian Rights (DPR), U.N. Committee on the Exercise of the Inalienable Rights of the Palestinian People, *The Origins and Evolution of the Palestine Problem: 1917-1988*, June 30, 1990, available online at the U.N. CEIRPP website: http://www.un.org/depts/dpa/qpal/committee.htm. See the report for further discussion and sources.
[3] Michael B. Oren, *Power, Faith, and Fantasy: America in the Middle East 1776 to Present* (New York: W.W. Norton & Company, Inc., 2007) p. 401.
[4] Theodor Herzl, *Complete Diaries*, ed. Raphael Patai, trans. Harry Zohn (New York: Herzl Press and T. Yoseloff, 1960), vol. I, p. 88, cited in Edward W. Said, *The Question of Palestine* (New York: Vintage Books Edition, 1992), p. 13.
[5] Theodor Herzl, *The Jewish State* (Dover Publications, New York, 1988), pp. 69, 95-96, 98, 123, available online at the Project Gutenberg website: http://www.gutenberg.org/files/25282/25282-h/25282-h.htm. See the website for further information on the translated edition. *Der Judenstaat* was originally published on February 14, 1896.
[6] Said, p. 97.
[7] Sir John Hope Simpson, C.I.E., *Report on Immigration, Land Settlement and Development*, October 1930 ("The Hope Simpson Report"), available online at the UNISPAL website: http://domino.un.org/unispal.nsf.
[8] Benny Morris, "The Tangled Truth," *The New Republic*, May 7, 2008: http://www.tnr.com/story.html?id=0e100478-298c-438c-a994-e1800474ad19&p=1; Said, p. 23, 98.
[9] Rabbi Jon-Jay Tilsen, *Ottoman Land Registration Law as a Contributing Factor in the Israeli-Arab Conflict*, Congregation Beth El-Keser Israel (BEKI): http://www.beki.org/landlaw.html (accessed

February 18, 2009). See the website for further discussion and sources.

[10] *Ha'aretz*, April 4, 1969, cited in Said, p. 14.

[11] *Documents From Israel, 1967-1973: Readings for a Critique of Zionism*, ed. Uri Davis and Norton Mezvinsky (London: Ithaca Press, 1975), p. 44. cited in Said, p. 14.

[12] Chaim Weizmann, *Trial and Error* (New York, Harper, 1949), pp. 177-178, 181, cited in *The Origins and Evolution of the Palestine Problem: 1917-1988*.

[13] Letter from British Foreign Minister Arthur James Balfour to Lord Rothschild, November 2, 1917 (The "Balfour Declaration"), available online at the Yale Avalon Project website.

[14] Said, p. 13.

[15] Yosef Heller, *Bama'avak Lamdina* (Jerusalem, 1985), p. 140, cited in Noam Chomsky, *Fateful Triangle: The United States, Israel & The Palestinians* (Cambridge, MA: South End Press, 1999) p.481.

[16] Said, p. 26-28.

[17] *The Origins and Evolution of the Palestine Problem: 1917-198*.

[18] Oren, *Power, Faith, and Fantasy*, pp. 89, 348, 350, 352-366; Donald Neff, *Fallen Pillars: U.S. Policy towards Palestine and Israel since 1945*, excerpted at the *Washington Post* website: http://www.washingtonpost.com/wp-srv/style/longterm/books/chap1/fallenpillars.htm (accessed April 2, 2009).

[19] The King-Crane Commission report of 1919, available online at the Israel/Palestine Center for Research and Information website: http://www.ipcri.org/files/kingcrane.html.

[20] "Crane and King's Long-Hid Report on the Near East," *New York Times*, December 3, 1922.

[21] Christopher Sykes, *Crossroads to Israel, 1917-1948* (1965; reprinted Bloomington, Ind.: Indiana University Press, 1973), p. 5, cited by Said, p. 16, and Chomsky, p. 90. See also *The Origins and Evolution of the Palestine Problem: 1917-1988*.

[22] London, H.M. Stationary Office, *Palestine. Disturbances in May, 1921. Reports of the Commission of Inquiry with Correspondence Relating Thereto*, October 1921 ("The Haycraft Commission of Inquiry Report"), available online at the Internet Archive: http://www.archive.org/details/palestinedisturb00grearich.

The Rejection of Palestinian Self-Determination

23 Said, p.17
24 Chomsky, pp. 40, 91
25 *The Origins and Evolution of the Palestine Problem: 1917-1988.*
26 British White Paper of June 1922, available online at the Yale Avalon Project website.
27 United Nations Special Committee on Palestine, Report to the General Assembly, Volume I, September 3, 1947 (hereafter "UNSCOP Report"), available online at the United Nations Information System on the Question of Palestine (UNISPAL) website: http://domino.un.org/unispal.nsf. The quote is from an address to the House of Commons by Winston Churchill on May 23, 1939.
28 David Waines, "The Failure of the Nationalist Resistance," in *The Transformation of Palestine*, ed. Ibrahim Abu-Lughod (Evanston, Ill.: Northwestern University Press, 1971), p.220, cited by Said, p.83.
29 *The Covenant of the League of Nations*, available online at the Yale Avalon Project website.
30 *The Origins and Evolution of the Palestine Problem: 1917-1988.*
31 *The Palestine Mandate of the Council of the League of Nations*, July 24, 1922, available online at the Yale Avalon Project website.
32 *The Origins and Evolution of the Palestine Problem: 1917-1988.*
33 Nadav Shragai, "Descendants of 1929 massacre survivors bought Hebron house", *Haaretz*, December 27, 2007: http://www.haaretz.com/hasen/spages/938334.html; Nissan Ratzlav-Katz, "We Didn't Start the Fire", *National Review Online*, August 23, 2002: http://www.nationalreview.com/comment/comment-ratzlav-katz082302.asp; Shira Schoenberg, "The Hebron Massacre of 1929", *Jewish Virtual Library*: http://www.jewishvirtuallibrary.org/jsource/History/hebron29.html; Morris, "The Tangled Truth"; Chomsky, p. 90.
34 Report of the Commission on the Palestine Disturbances of August 1929 ("The Shaw Commission Report"), cited in *The Origins and Evolution of the Palestine Problem: 1917-1988.*
35 Sir John Hope Simpson, C.I.E., "Report on Immigration, Land Settlement and Development", October 1930 ("The Hope Simpson Report"), available online at the UNISPAL website.
36 Letter from Ramsay MacDonald to Chaim Weizmann, February 13, 1931 (The MacDonald Letter), available online at the UNISPAL website.

37 Chaim Weizmann, *Trial and Error* (New York, Harper, 1949), p. 335, cited in *The Origins and Evolution of the Palestine Problem: 1917-1988*.
38 *The Origins and Evolution of the Palestine Problem: 1917-1988*.
39 Simha Flapan, *Zionism and the Palestinians* (Barnes & Noble, New York, 1979) p. 134, cited in Chomsky, p. 51.
40 *London Sunday Times*, June 15, 1969, cited in Chomsky, p. 51.
41 Benny Morris, *1948: A History of the First Arab-Israeli War* (Yale University Press, 2008), excerpted from "An excerpt from Benny Morris's new book, '1948'", *Jerusalem Post*, May 7, 2008: http://www.jpost.com/servlet/Satellite?pagename=JPost%2FJPArticle%2FShowFull&cid=1209627033313.
42 Flapan, p.141-2, cited in Chomsky, p.91-92.
43 "Eichmann Tells His Own Damning Story", *Life*, Vol. 49, No. 22, November 28, 1960, p. 22, 146, available online at http://www.einsatzgruppenarchives.com/trials/profiles/confession.html.
44 Morris, "The Tangled Truth".
45 *The Origins and Evolution of the Palestine Problem: 1917-1988*
46 "Tegart's Wall", *Time*, June 20, 1983: http://www.time.com/time/magazine/article/0,9171,788709,00.html.
47 Report of the Palestine Royal Commission, July 1937 ("The Peel Commission Report"), available online at the UNISPAL website: http://domino.un.org/UNISPAL.NSF.
48 Christopher Sykes, *Crossroads to Israel: 1917-1948* (Indiana, Bloomington, 1965), p. 174-5, cited in Chomsky, p. 162 (on Zionist territorial ambitions also see p. 161); *The Origins and Evolution of the Palestine Problem: 1917-1988*.
49 *New Outlook* (Tel Aviv), April 1977, from Ben-Gurion's *Memoirs*, cited in Chomsky, p. 161.
50 Flapan, pp. 255-6, cited in Chomsky, p. 161.
51 Michael Bar-Zohar, *Ben-Gurion: A Biography* (Delacorte, New York, 1978), pp. 91-2, cited in Chomsky, p. 162. For a portion of the quote omitted by Chomsky on forming an army, citing the same source, see also http://qumsiyeh.org/whyactingisimportant/.
52 *The Origins and Evolution of the Palestine Problem: 1917-1988*. Also see the UNSCOP Report.

53 I use the term "anti-Semitism" here as it is most typically used, with regard to Jews. It should be noted, however, that Arabs are also Semitic people and therefore the term "anti-Semite" applies equally to racism against Arabs as against Jews. The British views towards the majority Arab population in Palestine, for instance, were extremely anti-Semitic.

54 The Alexandria Protocol, October 7, 1944, available online at the Yale Avalon Project: http://avalon.law.yale.edu/20th_century/alex.asp.

55 Pact of the League of Arab States, March 22, 1945, available online at the Yale Avalon Project: http://avalon.law.yale.edu/20th_century/arableag.asp.

56 Donald Neff, *Fallen Pillars: U.S. Policy towards Palestine and Israel since 1945*, excerpted at the *Washington Post* website: http://www.washingtonpost.com/wp-srv/style/longterm/books/chap1/fallenpillars.htm (accessed April 2, 2009).

57 Letter From President Roosevelt to King Ibn Saud, April 5, 1945, available online at the Yale Avalon Project: http://avalon.law.yale.edu/20th_century/decad161.asp.

58 Richard H. Curtis

59 Anglo-American Committee of Inquiry Report to the United States Government and His Majesty's Government in the United Kingdom, April 20, 1946, available online at the Yale Avalon Project: http://avalon.law.yale.edu/subject_menus/angtoc.asp.

60 "Immigration into Palestine – Statement by President Truman", October 4, 1946, available online at the Yale Avalon Project: http://avalon.law.yale.edu/20th_century/decad163.asp.

61 U.N. General Assembly Resolution 106, May 15, 1947, available online at the U.N. website: http://www.un.org. The Special Committee on Palestine consisted of representatives from Australia, Canada, Czechoslovakia, Guatemala, India, Iran, Netherlands, Peru, Sweden, Uruguay and Yugoslavia. Also see the U.N. website for membership information. Two states were admitted membership in 1947, Pakistan, and Yemen, both admitted in September, bringing the total to 57 members.

62 UNSCOP Report.

[63] "Background Story on Palestine Report", U.N. Department of Public Information Press Release, August 31, 1947, available online at the UNISPAL website.
[64] UNSCOP Report.
[65] "Background Story on Palestine Report".
[66] UNSCOP Report.
[67] From a map entitled "Palestine Land Ownership by Sub-Districts" showing 1945 statistics, United Nations, August 1950, available online at: http://domino.un.org/maps/m0094.jpg. Statistics were as follows (Arab versus Jewish land ownership in percentages): Safad: 68/18; Acre: 87/3; Tiberias: 51/38; Haifa: 42/35; Nazareth: 52/28; Beisan: 44/34; Jenin: 84/1, Tulkarm: 78/17; Nablus: 87/1; Jaffa: 47/39; Ramle: 77/14; Ramallah: 99/less than 1; Jerusalem: 84/2; Gaza: 75/4; Hebron: 96/less than 1; Beersheeba: 15/less than 1
[68] UNSCOP report.
[69] Article 49 of the Fourth Geneva Convention states that "The Occupying Power shall not deport or transfer parts of its own civilian population into the territory it occupies." One could argue that the letter of the law does not prohibit the transfer of parts of a civilian population that was *not* "its own", but such a legalistic interpretation in clear violation of the spirit of the law would be difficult to take seriously. The obvious intent is that the geo-political status of the territory not be reconstituted in a manner prejudicial to the rights of its inhabitants and that no attempts to colonize the occupied territory should occur.
[70] UNSCOP Report.
[71] International Court of Justice, "Advisory Opinion regarding the Status of South-West Africa", *ICJ Reports*. (1950), p. 132, cited in "The Origins and Evolution of the Palestine Problem: 1917-1988".
[72] UNSCOP Report.
[73] United States Position on Palestine Question, Statement by Herschel V. Johnson, United States Deputy Representative to the United Nations, October 11, 1947, available online at the Yale Avalon Project: http://avalon.law.yale.edu/20th_century/decad164.asp.
[74] U.N. General Assembly Resolution 181, November 29, 1947, available at the U.N. website.
[75] "Israel at the UN: Progress Amid a History of Bias", Anti-Defamation League, September 2008:

http://www.adl.org/international/Israel-UN-1-introduction.asp; Nicholas Hirshon, "Rare footage of UN vote creating Israel to screen at Flushing synagogue", *New York Daily News*, November 20, 2007: http://www.nydailynews.com/ny_local/queens/2007/11/20/2007-11-20_rare_footage_of_un_vote_creating_israel_.html. These are random examples. For another, take the BBC website, which shows a map of the UN partition plan above a heading that reads "Israel founded: UN partition plan". The text notes that the plan "was never implemented", which can hardly be reconciled with the assertion that the plan "founded" Israel, and yet there it is: http://news.bbc.co.uk/2/shared/spl/hi/middle_east/03/v3_israel_palestinians/maps/html/israel_founded.stm (accessed March 23, 2009). For a final example, take Michael B. Oren, *Power, Faith, and Fantasy: America in the Middle East, 1776 to the Present* (W. W. Norton & Company, New York, 2007), p. xxii. In his chronology, for the year 1947, Oren writes, "The United States, along with thirty-two other nations, votes in favor of UN Resolution 181, *partitioning Palestine into independent Arab and Jewish states*" (emphasis added). Oren certainly must know better, but makes the false statement anyway.

[76] Richard H. Curtis, "Truman Adviser Recalls May 14, 1948 US Decision to Recognize Israel", Washington Report on Middle East Affairs, May/June 1991, Page 17: http://www.washington-report.org/backissues/0591/9105017.htm.

[77] Donald Neff, "Rabin's Murder Rooted in Zionism's Violent Legacy", *Washington Report on Middle East Affairs*, January 1996; pp. 59-61: http://www.wrmea.com/backissues/0196/9601059.html.

[78] Yitzhak Shamir biography from the The Jewish Agency for Israel website: http://www.jafi.org.il/education/100/people/BIOS/shamir.html (accessed July 27, 2009).

[79] Donald Neff

[80] The official Irgun website: http://www.etzel.org.il/english/people/frame.htm (accessed July 27, 2009).

[81] British Government, *The Political History of Palestine* (Memorandum to the United Nations Special Committee on

Palestine)(Jerusalem, 1947), pp. 31-32, cited in *The Origins and Evolution of the Palestine Problem: 1917-1988*.
[82] British Government, *Palestine: Statement Relating to Acts of Violence*, Cmd. 6873 (1946), p. 3, cited in *The Origins and Evolution of the Palestine Problem: 1917-1988*.
[83] Donald Neff
[84] Ibid.
[85] Ibid.
[86] The Declaration of the Establishment of the State of Israel, May 14, 1948:
http://www.mfa.gov.il/MFA/Peace+Process/Guide+to+the+Peace+Process/Declaration+of+Establishment+of+State+of+Israel.htm.
[87] Shlomo Ben-Ami, "A War to Start All Wars", *Foreign Affairs*, September/October 2008:
http://www.foreignaffairs.com/articles/63585/shlomo-ben-ami/a-war-to-start-all-wars.

Made in the USA
San Bernardino, CA
25 April 2013